£2.33

WITHDRAWN

D0309342

BRITISH NEWSPAPERS

A HISTORY
AND GUIDE FOR
COLLECTORS

John Wilkes, M.P., champion of a free press able to report the proceedings of Parliament, arrested in 1763 on a charge of seditious libel. Drawn from life and etched in aqua-fortis by William Hogarth (see page 55).

BRITISH NEWSPAPERS

A HISTORY
AND GUIDE FOR COLLECTORS

BRIAN LAKE

Introduction by
JOHN FROST

LONDON: SHEPPARD PRESS

Published by
SHEPPARD PRESS LIMITED
Russell Chambers, Covent Garden
London WC2E 8AX

First edition April 1984

ISBN: 0 900661 33 X

© BRIAN LAKE 1984

MADE IN ENGLAND
Typeset for the publishers by TRINTYPE
Printed by NENE LITHO
and bound by WOOLNOUGH BOOKBINDING
Wellingborough, Northamptonshire.

CONTENTS

FOREWORD

This is the first book to be published with the specific emphasis on *collecting* historical newspapers.

It has been written in response to a growing interest and will in turn help to focus attention on a generally unappreciated area on the margins of the book collecting world.

In the late eighteenth and early nineteenth centuries, Charles Burney, a wealthy classical scholar, amassed a collection of some 14,000 early printed books. When this collection was purchased by the nation and deposited in the British Museum in 1818, Burney's collection of British newspapers was also acquired, perhaps more by luck than good judgement. Since supplemented by further acquisitions it is now regarded as the finest collection in the world. Without the initial enthusiasm of a collector this would not be the case.

John Frost, who has provided the majority of the illustrations for this book, began collecting modern newspapers in the 1930s. The collection he has accumulated is now used by publishers, television, film companies and newspapers themselves as a unique loan service, and source of reference.

Teachers have begun to realise the special way in which newspapers reporting past events bring history to life, and as booksellers, collectors and librarians change their traditional attitude towards newspapers, and cease seeing them as an awkward encumbrance, difficult to store or display, they will take their proper place as an important element in the assessment of history.

The book is divided into two main sections. The first provides background information on the development of the press, without pretending to be comprehensive, but with comparative glances at newspapers in other parts of the English-speaking world. The second section aims to stimulate and inform those who are, or would like to be, newspaper collectors.

5

THE AUTHOR

Brian Lake was born in 1947 and from an early age seemed destined for a career in the world of newspapers and publishing. At the age of twelve he wrote, edited, produced and distributed, a school Gazette. Later at York University he read Social Science, but spent rather more of his time writing for, and editing, the university newspaper. After gaining a degree and valuable experience 'in print' he worked on several magazines and journals, including *Collectors' Weekly.* His interest in the history of journalism developed while editing *Great Newspapers Reprinted,* a highly successful series of facsimile reproductions of newspapers that reported historic events, from the Relief of Mafeking to V.E. Day.

In 1970 with a partner, he established the firm of Jarndyce Antiquarian Booksellers in Covent Garden, London, which has become one of the leading specialists in nineteenth century English Literature and, of course, in early newspapers and books on journalism.

ACKNOWLEDGE-MENTS

I would like to thank the following for particular help in compiling this book: John Frost, from whose collection of historic newspapers most of the illustrations have been taken; Robert Heron of the Original and Rare Newspaper Company, Covent Garden, for permission to reproduce items from his personal collection on pages 18, 26, 28, 32, 34, 36, 37, 38, 40, 51, 52, 104 and 106; Jeff Towns of Dylan's Bookstore, Swansea, for his help in finding the scarce *Times* misprint and contemporary report on pages 168 and 169; John and Vanessa Lindsay-Smith; Edith Finer of Frognal Rare Books; Helen Smith; The British Library Newspaper Library; the National Library of Wales; the St. Bride Printing Library; Trefor Rendall Davies of the Sheppard Press; Janet, William and Edward, and all the ladies and gentlemen of the press who made it possible.

B.L.

INTRODUCTION
BY JOHN FROST

It had been an uneventful shift. The time was now 2am on Sunday 5th October 1930.

Journalists on the *Sunday Express* were getting ready to pack it in for the night, when news came over the wire — forty-five people burned to death on the maiden voyage of the largest thing ever to fly, the R101 airship. It had crashed into a hillside in northern France.

The *Sunday Express* had a scoop. "Late Stop" on the paper decided to put through an edition, recalling writers and printers who had already gone to bed. Within three hours of the crash a special edition was on the streets. The news was being read throughout Britain while the embers were still cooling in France.

My first memory of newspaper collecting was of going out on that Sunday to buy a copy of the *News of the World* which also produced a "special" edition.

There isn't a scoop like the story of R101 every day. There are relatively few, in fact, in the 25,000 newspapers I have collected subsequently, but every day, in virtually every country in the world, newspapers are on sale with some dramatic story hours, minutes even, after the event. Aided extensively now by the same technology that brings television and wireless to people instantaneously, newspapers are essentially the same as they have been for a century-and-a-half. They still, and will always have to, rely on machinery to produce a concrete endproduct, and after all the rush to get the product on sale, they are discarded quicker than almost any other commodity.

The importance of the newspaper lies in this urgency and immediacy. Through its pages arrives the first opportunity to take in information, reflect and then form an opinion of what has been read. Without pretending that newspapers always provide the right facts, or the right interpretation of events as they happen, they do provide something which is much more important, a chronicle of history *as it is being made*. The

7

The R 101 Crashes And Is Destroyed: Lord Thomson, Sir Sefton Brancker And 44 Others Burned To Death.

THE TRAGIC AFTERMATH.—Dead bodies shrouded in sheets near the wrecked airship.— *Special "Daily Express" Picture.*

GREAT AIRSHIP STRIKES A HILL AFTER BATTLE WITH A STORM.

SLEEPING PASSENGERS ENVELOPED BY SWIFTLY RUSHING FLAMES

WHAT WAS THE CAUSE?

AIRSHIP IN PERIL THREE MONTHS

The Last Message: "Going To Bed."

The last of a series of wireless messages received at Le Bourget from the R 101, states Reuter, was timed 1.38 a.m. Eleven minutes

Daily Herald

ON YOUR FEET FOR HOURS ? Then Don't Forget That ZAM-BUK Removes Pain, Soreness & Cores

SAUSAGES GO BETTER WITH H·P SAUCE

No. 7140   MONDAY, SEPTEMBER 4, 1939   ONE PENNY

WAR DECLARED BY BRITAIN AND FRANCE

The Fleet Moves Into Position

GREAT BRITAIN DECLARED WAR ON GERMANY AT 11 O'CLOCK YESTERDAY MORNING.

Six hours later, at 5 p.m., France declared war.

Britain's resolution to defend Poland against Nazi aggression was described by the newly-formed Ministry of Information in one of its first announcements, as follows:—

"At 11.15 this morning (Sunday) Mr R Dunbar Head of the Treaty Department of the Foreign Office, went to the German Embassy, where he was received by Dr Kordt, the Charge d'Affairs.

"Mr Dunbar handed to Dr Kordt a notification that a state of war existed between Great Britain and Germany as from 11 A.M. B.S.T. On receiving the notification the constituted the formal declaration of war.

Navy Fully Mobilised

Unthinkable We Should Refuse The Challenge

– THE KING.

Broadcasting last evening from his study at Buckingham Palace, the King said:

IN this grave hour, perhaps the most fatal in our history, I send to every household of my people, both at home and overseas, this message, spoken with the same depth of feeling for each one of you as if I were able to cross your threshold and speak to you myself.

For the second time in the lives of most of us we are at war.

Over and over again we have tried to find a peaceful way out of the differences be-

WAR CABINET OF

POLES SMASH WAY INTO E. PRUSSIA

OFFICIALS in Warsaw stated late last night that the Polish army has smashed a way across the Northern border into East Prussia, after driving the Germans from several Polish towns in bitter fighting.

On the Northern Front the Poles are reported to have defeated the German effort to drive a barrier across the upper part of the Corridor. The Germans fell back behind their frontiers.

The Poles say they have broken through the German fortifications as far as the railway terminus of Deutsch Eylau.

Early to-day an official Polish communiqué admitted that Polish troops had been compelled to abandon Czenstochowa, 48 miles from Deutsch Eylau, after heavy fighting.

London Hears Its First Raid Warning

LONDON was calm yesterday when it heard its first air raid warning.

This is the official statement issued by the Air Ministry:—

At 11.30 a.m. yesterday an aircraft was observed approaching the South

An air warning could not be readily determined and an air raid warning was

BLACK-OUT TIME TO-NIGHT—7.10

Continued on Page 1, Earlier fighting details on Page 10

8

story, as written in the newspaper of the day is, for most people, the reality of the situation. A slick headline becomes someone else's opinion. "It was in the papers. It must be true."

Looking back at yesterday's papers gives an insight into how the public received the news at the time. This, to me, is at the heart of the reasons why newspapers are so stimulating.

As an example of this, papers reporting the outbreak of the Second World War are particularly evocative. There is no way of getting closer to the experience, or bringing it back vividly to mind than picking up a newspaper with the front-page news: "FIRST DAY OF THE SECOND GREAT WAR . . . 'We fight against evil things — brute force, bad faith, injustice, oppression and persecution — and against them I am certain that the right will prevail,' the Premier said."

Balanced against such reports of the important moments in history, there are times when "stories" which have covered a front page are later proved to be the result of a false lead, or are just plainly inaccurate. On 1 February 1970 *The People* banner headline read: "HORROR IN A NAMELESS VILLAGE — British Guilt Revealed." The story unveiled a massacre of twenty-five suspected terrorists by British troops in Malaya in 1948, and caused a political stir at the time. Exactly six months later this seven-line "filler" appeared in the *Daily Mail*: "A Scotland Yard investigator has found that charges in a Sunday newspaper that members of a patrol of Scots Guards massacred twenty-five suspected terrorists in the Malay jungles in 1948 were unfounded."

The importance of this example is not that the incident did or did not take place. It was a controversy created by a newspaper; a piece of history that will not be found in history books, only the papers of the time.

Opposite:
DAILY EXPRESS
No. 9493
October 6, 1930
(578 x 405mm)

DAILY HERALD
No. 7349
September 4, 1939
(540 x 425mm)

There will be no war

Ambassador flies back, finds Berlin cheerful

There will be no European war.

Why?

Because the decision of peace and war depends on one man, the German Führer. And he will not be responsible for making war at present.

Hitler has shown himself throughout his career to be a man of exceptional astuteness. Both at the time when he was a struggling politician in Germany and since he has become the master of Germany, he has been remarkably accurate in his estimates of the movements of public opinion, the strength of different forces, and the trend of events.

These qualities, exercised in the situation today, will guide Hitler towards peace.

For if the Czechs fail to make the necessary concessions to the Germans in Czecho-Slovakia, the French and the Russians will not come to their aid. And in that case the danger of a European war is over.

1914-1938

And if the Czechs (after making the necessary concessions) are supported by the French and the Russians in resistance to Germany, then, of course, the

Sir Nevile Henderson, British Ambassador to Berlin, flew back to Germany last night after the London talks, and found an optimistic spirit at the Embassy. Sir Nevile is pictured here—diplomatically avoiding an inquisitive spectator—on his way to see Lord Halifax at the Foreign Office yesterday.

RIBBENTROP SEES OUR ENVOY TODAY

SIR NEVILE HENDERSON, British Ambassador in Ger-

the atmosphere much easier than when he made his secret

'There will be no war' — said Lord Beaverbrook in 1938. An unsuccessful attempt by a newspaper proprietor to influence the course of history.

Occasionally, newspapers help to make history. The Spanish-American War of 1898 was dubbed the "Newspapers' War" because of its exploitation by American newspaper proprietors to boost circulations. Randolph Hearst, the legendary press king, owner at that time of the *San Francisco Examiner* and the *New York Journal*, decided that the American people wanted war with Spain over Cuba, and he wanted more readers for his papers. When one of his artists asked to be recalled from Cuba because of the lack of activity, Hearst cabled: "Please remain. You furnish the pictures and I'll furnish the war." The war happened. In the year before World War II, Lord Beaverbrook's *Daily Express* proclaimed: 'No War, This Year or Next'. His attempt at influencing the course of events was rather less effective than Hearst's, but the efforts both resulted in coloured, but colourful, journalism.

Where newspapers come into their own, I believe, is on the occasions when they report events which subsequently do get into the history books. They provide *real* colour through their style, language, pictures, of what it was like to be there.

As well as being historically interesting, newspapers are a form of entertainment. The paper is the first thing to turn to in the morning, a relaxing and easy way to take in information, broken up in to accessible compartments and with visual stimulation from advertisements, cartoons, photographs and puzzles. True of today's papers, this is even more so of those from the past. Reprints in recent years have even put historic headlines back on to the news-stands. "HITLER DEAD" is a strong front page lead story, but with the whole newspaper in front of you, the reader becomes quickly engrossed in the more day-to-day details of living in 1945, a day or so before the end of War in Europe, when a B.S.A. bicycle cost £8 19s 6d, Marconiphone was the "Real Thing" in radio and Mars Bars were transformed into delicious Mars potato rock buns . . .

11

$50,000 REWARD.—WHO DESTROYED THE MAINE?—$50,000 REWARD.

EDITION FOR GREATER NEW YORK

NEW YORK JOURNAL
AND ADVERTISER.

NEW YORK, THURSDAY, FEBRUARY 17, 1898.—16 PAGES.

PRICE ONE CENT

DESTRUCTION OF THE WAR SHIP MAINE WAS THE WORK OF AN ENEMY.

$50,000!
$50,000 REWARD!
**For the Detection of the
Perpetrator of
the Maine Outrage!**

W. R. HEARST.

Assistant Secretary Roosevelt Convinced the Explosion of the War Ship Was Not an Accident.

The Journal Offers $50,000 Reward for the Conviction of the Criminals Who Sent 258 American Sailors to Their Death. Naval Officers Unanimous That the Ship Was Destroyed on Purpose.

$50,000!
$50,000 REWARD!
**For the Detection of the
Perpetrator of
the Maine Outrage!**

W. R. HEARST.

NAVAL OFFICERS THINK THE MAINE WAS DESTROYED BY A SPANISH MINE.

Hidden Mine or a Sunken Torpedo Believed to Have Been the Weapon Used Against the American Man-of-War---Officers and Men Tell Thrilling Stories of Being Blown Into the Air Amid a Mass of Shattered Steel and Exploding Shells---Survivors Brought to Key West Scout the Idea of Accident---Spanish Officials Protest Too Much---Our Cabinet Orders a Searching Inquiry---Journal Sends Divers to Havana to Report Upon the Condition of the Wreck.
Was the Vessel Anchored Over a Mine?

BY CAPTAIN E. L. ZALINSKI, U. S. A.

(Captain Zalinski is the inventor of the famous dynamite gun, which would be the principal factor in our coast defence in case of war.)

Assistant Secretary of the Navy Theodore Roosevelt says he is convinced that the destruction of the Maine in Havana Harbor was not an accident. The Journal offers a reward of $50,000 for exclusive evidence that will convict the person, persons or Government criminally responsible for the destruction of the American battle ship and the death of 258 of its crew.

The suspicion that the Maine was deliberately blown up grows stronger every hour. Not a single fact to the contrary has been produced. Captain Sigsbee, of the Maine, and Consul-General Lee both urge that public opinion be suspended until they have completed their investigation. They are taking the course of tactful men who are convinced that there has been treachery.

Washington reports very late that Captain Sigsbee had feared some such event as a hidden mine. The English cipher code was used all day yesterday by the naval officers in cabling instead of the usual American code.

12

Taking a wider perspective over the last 250 years, as I am able to do with a collection of newspapers which goes back to the 1630s, and looking at original issues from, say, fifty different years and several countries, a picture begins to emerge of the development in presentation of news. Small broadsides, printed by hand on one side of the page only, growing into the "acres of unrelieved print" of the machine-printed papers of the nineteenth century; headlines slowly expanding, eventually filling the page; typefaces changing; line illustrations introduced and then supplemented by photographs; punchiness replacing the convoluted sentences of the crusty

Opposite:
NEW YORK JOURNAL
February 17, 1898
Randolph Hearst provoking war with Spain after the sinking of the MAINE.
(510 x 380mm, taken from a reprint).

Right:
DAILY MIRROR
May 2, 1945

13

Right:
EVENING STANDARD
No. 29428
November 11, 1918
(450 x 320mm)

Victorian papers; the increasing subtlety of the advertisements; the introduction of different kinds of newsprint and printing methods — all these things and more build into a picture that reflects, perhaps better than anything else, the year-to-year changes in society, fashions, attitudes, politics and economics.

Introducing the concept of "collecting" historic newspapers to a wider audience, as I hope I am doing here, is a difficult task. "Old" doesn't always mean "waste", but try and explain that to the man on the Clapham omnibus who thinks nothing more of his morning purchase than leaving it on the seat when he gets off. At the moment, there are very few collectors. Interest has been increased by the availability of reprinted papers, but widespread realisation of the possibilities of collecting originals is still in the future. The scope is immense, the possibilities for specialising in particular sorts of papers, events, periods of history, countries, unlimited.

The main concern of this book is interest in original newspapers as objects of history, rather than as an investment, but it is true to say that they are generally not expensive. Even though the earlier papers — before 1750 (when offered for sale) — are not always cheap, a good collection of originals will not cost the earth. Much of my own collection has been obtained by exchanging with other collectors around Britain and the world.

So, without completely accepting Lord Macaulay's epigram that "the only true history of a country is to be found in its newspapers" and maintaining a critical eye on the writings of the journalist's pen, there is a wealth of largely unexplored entertainment and information. Yesterday's papers, it is said, are only good enough to wrap the fish and chips, but an American journalist (with an eye for a neat turn of phrase) put it another way: "The fish seller wraps fish in paper. We wrap news in paper. The content is what counts not the wrapper."

HISTORY OF THE NEWSPAPER

A Newspaper is a regularly published journal containing news, advertisements and other information of public interest. Most modern papers can be divided into 'tabloids' such as the *Mirror* or 'broadsheets' such as the *Guardian*. The earlier history of newspapers must include publications described by alternative names — newsbooks, newsletters, newspamphlets and broadsides, some of which were 'one-off' publications. Magazines, specialised and containing little topical material that can be described as news, are a separate area of interest although up to the middle of the eighteenth century their history is entwined with that of the newspaper.

This first section of the book concentrates on the historical development of printed news, and provides an essential background to the collecting of newspapers, which is the subject of part two.

Availability of originals to the present-day collector is affected by a number of factors. In the earliest period (1500-1640) it is fair to say that examples are still obtainable, but not readily so. However from the English Civil War onwards, the serious collector will be able to locate copies of most of newspapers mentioned, though issues covering specific events may well prove elusive. The illustrations are, in the main, of the newspapers that can be obtained by collectors.

1500-1640 ORIGINS: CORANTOS AND INTELLIGENCERS

Stanley Morison, perhaps the foremost historian of the newspaper, wrote that its origins "can hardly be taken far beyond the beginning of the sixteenth century" and discounts "all ancient analogies to the news." It is only necessary to say that both the Chinese and Romans had an "official press" that consisted of officially approved reports of events.

In Europe, from the fifth century to the fifteenth, the dissemination of the written word became virtually extinct, but trade in the big commercial centres of Venice, Antwerp, Frank-

VOX POPVLI.

OR

NEVVES FROM SPAYNE,

tranſlated according to the Spaniſh coppie.

Which may ſerve to forewarn both England
and the United Provinces how farre
to truſt to Spaniſh pretences.

Imprinted in the yeare 1620.

Opposite:
NEWES FROM SPAYNE
1620
(190 x 145mm)
More political comment than news: a 'report' of the imagined insults received by Charles, Prince of Wales on his visit to Spain, written by Thomas Scott, published in London.

furt, Augsburg and Strasbourg encouraged its revival. International fairs in these cities became focus-points of "news exchange". Private letters on trade and politics slowly turned into more public documents to be passed from hand to hand. Couriers who carries these letters became known as "Intelligencers" — providers of information on events, indulgences, proclamations, military feats, atrocities, marvels and monsters.

Stimulus for real "news" came from the Turkish Wars about the year 1500. The means of spreading the news to a wider audience was provided by Gutenberg's movable-type printing press in the mid-fifteenth century.

In 1502, the first report to appear with the word *Zeitung*, (newspaper) was published in Germany: *Neue Zeitung von Orient* which reported a victory over the Turks.

At this stage, as for many years after, setting up type was a laborious business and much of the communication in the sixteenth century remained in written form. Newsletters developed in Italy. Information collected from European cities was gathered together into bulletins which could be had on subscription. The role of overseas ambassadors for European countries included sending regular reports back to their sovereigns, so placing them somewhere between foreign correspondent and spy.

In Britain, booksellers took up the continental idea of the "Intelligencer" and employed scribes to write out sheets of interesting local information. The earliest known printed newspamphlet in Britain is the *Trewe Encountre* of 1513, an officially authorised four-page sheet to celebrate the defeat of the Scots at Flodden Field. It was illustrated with a woodcut and was headlined:

HEREAFTER ENSUE THE TREWE ENCOUNTRE OR BATAYLE LATELY DON BETWENE ENGLANDE AND SCOTLANDE AT WHICH BATAYLE THE SCOTTISHE KYNGE WAS SLAYNE

The certaine Newes

of this present Weeke.

BROVGHT BY SVNDRY

Posts from seuerall places, but chiefly
the progresse and arriuall of Count *Mansfield*
with the Duke of *Brunswicke* into *Champeney* in
FRANCE; and the ioyning of sundry of the
Princes with them, &c.

With the preparation of the French

King to resist him : And what great feare Count
MANSFIELDS vnexpected arriuall hath
put all FRANCE in, &c.

Out of the best Informations of Letters and
other, this second of August 1 6 2 2.

LONDON,
Printed by *I. H.* for *Nathaniel Butter*, and are to
be sold at his shop at the signe of the *Pide Bull*
at *S. Austins* Gate. 1622.

Newspamphlets such as this provided the only newspaper-type literature in Britain up to 1600. Typical was the heading:

Wonderful and Strange Newes out of Suffolk and Essex where it Rayned Wheat the Space of Six or Seven Miles

on a pamphlet of 1583. Less sensational information would be more simply entitled "Newes out of Kent", Suffolk, or wherever it might be. Between 1590 and 1610 some 500 of these pamphlets or newsbooks were published of which many are known today in title only. There was little regularity about their publication and only slight signs of common titles emerging, although some incorporated the words "True News", "Credible Report" and "True Relation".

On the continent of Europe, written newsletters slowly developed into more regular printed papers. Between 1590 and 1610 a number of weekly, monthly and six-monthly periodicals are recorded emanating from Antwerp, Strasbourg and Augsburg when, for the first time, publication was fixed by a period of time rather than in response to events as they happened. Words began to be used in regular titles that are recognisable in the names of modern newspapers: News, Gazette, Mercury, Courier, Intelligencer, Courant.

The first English-language newspaper appeared in 1620 in Amsterdam following Dutch and French *corantos* (currents of news) published in the city, and a few copies only survive headed *Corrant out of Italy, Germany, etc.* James I, king of England, continued the earlier tradition set by Elizabeth I of restricting any ephemeral publication likely to threaten the throne by issuing an edict prohibiting "all lavish and licentious talking in matters of State". But the Dutch-printed corantos still continued to appear in London and James reluctantly decided to allow publication in England in the hope that he could control, through licensing, what he had been previously unable to stop entering the country from abroad.

Opposite:
THE CERTAINE NEWES
1622
(240 x 155mm)
An early unnumbered newsbook printed by John Haviland and published by Nathaniel Butter.

21

A true Report of all the speciall

Passages of note lately happened in the Ile of Ree, betwixt the Lord Duke of *Buckingham* his Grace, Generall for the King of England, and Monsieur *Thorax*, Gouernour of the Fort in the said Ile, as also betwixt the Duke and the French King, likewise the present state of the Rochellers, and of the Kings Armie lying before it

Nouemb. 1.   *Numb.* 40.

The Continuation of our vveek-
ly *Newes* from the 24. of October to the 2. of *Nouember.*

Containing amongst the rest these speciall particulars following.

Vnto which is added Newes from *Germany*, *France*, and diuers parts of Christendome.

The warlike proceedings of the Imperialists, and *Danish*.

The Treatie of Peace betwixt *Poland* and *Sweden*.

The Empereurs Iourney towards Prage.

Besides diuers other matters of moment.

Printed by Authoritie.

LONDON
Printed for *Nathaniell Butter*, 1 6 2 7.

No. 40 of the Fifth series of The Weekly Newes, *the first numbered and dated newsbook.*

Corante, or, Newes from Italy, Germany, Hungarie, Spaine and France, London, printed for N.B. [probably Nathaniel Butter] September the 24 1621 is the earliest-dated English-printed newspaper of which copies survive. It lasted until 22 October of the same year — a short run of seven small folio single-sheet copies. In the following May, the first English newspaper was published in pamphlet form by Thomas Archer and Nicholas Bourne which has come to be known as the *Weekly Newes*. In October Archer and Bourne joined with Butter and the other publishers to turn the *Weekly Newes* into the first numbered and dated newspaper. Continuity was by date, while the title varied. More licences were granted by the Crown in 1622 & 1623 and the English newspaper was underway.

Because of the need for a licence in order to publish, and the king's sensitivity to home news, the content of these quarto-size papers was mainly a translation of information "lifted" from similar European publications. Typical is the following from an extant copy of the *Weekly Newes*:

> From Bergstrate the 14. of May is written the followeth, the former passed night, and yet continueth, the passing away of the Spanish Armie, with their artillery, and baggage wagons, through the Darmstratts Countrey to the Towne of Bensheym. pittifully spoyling the Countrey . . . From Wezell, the 18 of May it is written that Graue Henricke van berghe . . . hath made a bridge betwene this and Berke over the Rhine, to what end we yet understand not . . .

Opposite
A TRUE REPORT . . .
No. 40
November 1, 1639
(155 x 90mm)
No. 40 of the Fifth series of The Weekly Newes, *the first numbered and dated newsbook.*

Archer founded a periodical in opposition to his former partners between 1624 and 1628, while Butter and Bourne's newsbooks continued until 1632 when a Star Chamber decree of 17 October suppressed all such publications for a period of six years.

Upon consideracion had at the Board of the greate abuse in the printing and publishing of the ordenary Gazetts and Pamphletts of newes from forraigne partes, And upon signification of his majesties expresse pleasure and Commaund for the present suppressing of the same, It was thought fitt and hereby ordered that all printing and publishing of the same be accordingly supprest and inhibited . . .

Prior to 1632, attacks on the publishers of news came from other quarters. The dramatists of the day who, in their own way, had continued and extended the role of the Intelligencers in their plays, were jealous of what was clearly a change in public taste. Ben Jonson, Shirley, and Fletcher poured scorn on "all the cheats of the lying stationers" and the newswriters: "Captain Hungry who will write you a battle in any part of Europe at an hour's notice and yet never set foot outside a tavern". Fletcher wrote of correspondents who "writ a full hand gallop and wasted more harmless paper than ever did laxative physic".

Despite this opposition, and the ban imposed by the Star Chamber, Butter and Bourne still continued with *The Swedish Intelligencer*, though this was not strictly a newsbook, but a half-yearly digest. It provided a link through to the end of the Star Chamber ban in December 1638. Butter and Bourne clearly had satisfied the king of their loyalty, for they received at that time "Royal Letters Patent" for exclusive right to publish "all matter of History or Newes . . . Gazetts, Corrantos or Occurrences . . ." from abroad only, home news still being regarded as too sensitive for the attention of journalists.

Folke Dahl's *Bibliography of English Corantos and Periodical Newsbooks* 1620-1642 suggests that in this period about 1000 were published, while only 349 different issues were physically examined by Dahl. Of the 40,000 estimated copies printed only some 500-600 seem to have survived.

Dahl quotes the following written by Richard Braithwait in his *Whimzies, or a New Cast of Characters,* 1631, as the explanation for such a high rate of disappearance in his attack on a 'Corranto-coiner':

> our best comfort is, his *Chymeras (the newsbooks)* live not long; a weeke is the longest in the Citie, and after their arrivall, little longer in the Countrey, Which past, they melt like *Butter,* or match a pipe and so *Burne.* But indeede, most commonly it is the height of their ambition, to aspire to the imployment of stopping mustard-pots, or wrapping up papper, pouder, staves-aker, &c. which done, they expire.

Good Newes from

SOVTH-HAMPTON,

AND

BASINGSTOKE,

in *Hampshire.*

As it was related in a Letter from thence by one Mafter *Otter,*
to a Merchant of good quality, in Lumbardftreet.

With the Copy of a Letter fent by Captaine *Swanly,* Captaine
of one of the Kings Ships, to the Major and Com-
munalty of the faid Towne.

As alfo another Letter to the fame Merchint from *Bafingftoke,*
relating the paffages there.

LONDON,

Printed for *Tho. Bates,* and are to be fold at his fhop in the
Old Bayly. **1642.**

1640-1700
ESTABLISHMENT OF THE WEEKLY PRESS:

POLITICS AND RELIGION

From the Turkish Wars of 1500 to the Falklands War of 1982 battles between men have boosted the circulation of newspapers. This was particularly so of the English Civil War 1642-1651. The Star Chamber was abolished in 1641, and its disappearance meant an end to the licensing of publications. The abolition coincided with a public thirst for home news of the struggle between King and Commons rather than Butter and Bourne's "forreigne weekly avisoes" which, by all accounts, were not selling well. If sales did not improve, wrote Butter in 1640, "we shall be forced to put a period to the Presse and leave every man to the pleasing of his own fansie . . ."

In 1642, when Butter's Royal Patent from Charles I was terminated, the increased interest in home affairs was reflected in the title of one of his newsbooks: *A little true forraine newes better than a great deale of domestick spurious false newes published daily without feare or wit to the shame of the nation . . .*

The new-found freedom of the press had indeed fired the printers with energy, and imagination. Butter was referring to such items as *The Marine Mercurie,* or 'a true relation of the strange appearances of a Man-Fish, about Three miles within the River Thames, having a Mosket in one hand and a petition in the other', and *Newes, True Newes, Laudable Newes, Citie Newes, Countrie Newes, The World is Mad, or, It is a Mad World, Especially Now When, In the Antipodes, These Things Are Come to Pass,* both of 1642. Or this, from 1645: *No Newes, but a Letter to Everybody.*

Opposite:
GOOD NEWES FROM SOUTH-HAMPTON AND BASINGSTOKE
1642
(175 x 140mm)
Newsbooks reporting domestic events reappeared after the abolition of the Star Chamber in 1641.

What everybody wanted to read (all those who could) was of the goings-on in Parliament. These proceedings were taken down by newsletter writers and, with Parliament's permission, printed. It was with the inception of these *diurnals* that news began to appear on the front page of the publication under a regular title rather than on page 3 after the title page, as in most books.

THE
SCOTS
SCOVTS
DISCOVERIES

BY

THEIR LONDON

INTELLIGENCER.

And prefented to the Lords
of the Covenant of *Scotland*.
Anno Domini. 1639

LONDON,
Printed for *William Sheares*, 1642.

Samuel Peck, a scrivener, or scribe, with a booth in Westminster Hall, was the first to have his reports published under the title *The Heads of Several Proceedings in this Present Parliament. Diurnal Occurrences in Parliament* from 22 November to 29 November 1641. This was followed by a spate of diurnals through the period of Cromwell's rule, 350 in all up to 1665. Competition was intense. 'Take heede of a false and scandalous Diurnal fashioned by a Company of Grubstreet mercenary fellowes' complained one writer.

During the Civil War, countless newsbooks presented the positions of both sides, mainly under the titles of *Mercurius* or *Intelligencer*.

Most of them were small enough to be disposed of (eaten if necessary) by soldiers or camp followers when captured, to prevent information falling into the hands of the enemy. The bulk of the contents consisted, however, of "abuse, retort and propaganda, the main themes religion, politics and war". They were usually monthly (or thereabouts), some weekly and a very few thrice-weekly. 30,000 of them came out in less than twenty years up to 1660. *Mercurius Britanicus* was set up by Parliamentarians to counter the Royalist *Mercurius Aulicus* in 1643. Both sides tried to outdo each other in vituperation until 1655 when Cromwell became tired of being described as "Carrot-Nose" and "Beelzebub's Chief Ale-Brewer" and introduced anti-press ordinances reinforcing the ineffective licensing laws of 1647.

The anti-press laws had the effect of killing off the newsbooks, leaving only two official Parliamentarian papers: *Mercurius Politicus* (1650-1660) and the *Publick Intelligencer* (1655-1660) both produced by Cromwell's official journalist, Marchamont Nedham who had earlier edited *Mercurius Britanicus*. In 1647, two years after printing *A Hue and Cry after a Wilful King . . . which hath gone astray these four Years from his Parliament with a guilty Conscience, bloody*

Opposite:
THE SCOTS SCOUTS
DISCOVERIES
1642
(182 x 135mm)
One of the earliest newsbooks to report affairs in Scotland, published in London.

29

A PERFECT DIVRNALL OF THE PASSAGES In Parliament:

From the 16. of Ianuary to the 23 of Iannary,

Collected by the same hand that formerly drew up the Copy for William Cook of Furnifulls Inne, being now printed by I: Okes, Fr: Leach, and are to be sold by Fr: Coles in the Old Baily. 1642.

Munday the 16. of Ianuary.

THe Houſe of Commons having fully a-greed and concluded upon the propo-ſitions to be ſent to his Majeſty, they preſented them to the Lords at a con-ference deſiring their aſſent and con-currence with them, that they might be forthwith ſent to his Majeſty; the ſaid propoſitions was then read at a conference, their being 14. of them, the effect whereof being as hath beene formerly related for the ſetling of Re-ligion, by the paſſing of ſuch Bills as have beene, and are made ready by both Houſes for his Majeſties aſſent, that the proceſſes of Parliament may have a free courſe to the puniſhment of Delinquents, for the ſuppreſſing of

Ii   Popery

Hands, and a Heartfull of broken Vows and Protestations, Nedham changed sides for no apparent reason, begged Charles I's forgiveness and promptly established *Mercurius Pragmaticus* committed to the King's cause. Cromwell sought to suppress it and imprisoned Richard Lownes, the printer, and in 1649, Nedham. Within three months, Nedham had repented of his Royalist support.

In 1659 as the Long Parliament came to an end, a new Royalist newswriter, Henry Muddiman, took over from Nedham, who fled to Holland. Muddiman's papers were *Mercurius Publicus* (1660-1663) and the *Parliamentary Intelligencer* (1659-1663), which took over the government monopoly of the news. In May 1660, Charles II returned to England to be restored to the throne and within a month the new parliament enacted that 'no person whatsoever do presume at his peril to print any votes or proceedings of this House without the special leave and order of this House'. At the same time an act sought to stop abuses in printing and the position of Surveyor of the Imprimery, or Press, was established. Roger L'Estrange, a strong supporter of both the monarchy and a licensed press, took over this post in 1663. All printing offices in England, and vendors of books and papers were under his control. He was also one of the licensers of the press and had the sole privilege of writing, printing and publishing a newspaper — the *Intelligencer* (1663-1666) which appeared on the streets on Mondays; the Thursday supplement was *The Newes*. L'Estrange later helped found an early commercial paper the *City Mercury* in 1675 and the *Observator* in 1681.

L'Estrange's monopoly was broken from the most unlikely quarter. In 1665, while the Royal Court was in Oxford during the Great Plague in London, the *Oxford Gazette* was published there. After twenty three issues, and the King's return

Opposite:
A PERFECT DIURNALL OF THE PASSAGES IN PARLIAMENT
No. 3
January 16-23, 1642
(200 x 150mm)
Most distinctive of the 'diurnals' which reported proceedings in Parliament and one of the earliest to regularly use woodcut illustrations.

Mercurius Civicus.

LONDONS
INTELLIGENCER:
OR,
Truth impartially related from thence to the whole Kingdome, to
prevent mif-information.

From *Thurfday, Auguft* 3. to *Friday Auguft* 11. 1643.

 N the laft weekes Intelligence mention was made of a Proclamation iffued forth from *Oxford* in His Majefties name, wherein he forbids any traffique with, or bringing of any provifion into the City of *London*, fince which time there hath come forth from thence another Proclamation, much to the fame purpofe, though of a larger extent, in regard both of the perfons intended in it,

L   and

32

to London, the title changed to the *London Gazette*. It is perhaps the most famous of early newspapers; it is certainly the paper with the longest history as it is still published today as the official government informaton sheet. In its early years it consisted of a single quarto sheet printed on both sides in two columns giving mainly shipping news and short foreign advices.

Suppression of unlicensed news was reinforced in 1680 by a further proclamation which was firmly administered by the courts. One newspaper that managed to survive was *Heraclitus Ridens* (1681-1682), the first real satirical journal. A number of papers, with a heavily religious bias flourished in the early 1680s such as the *True Protestant Mercury* (1680-1681).

With the arrival of William of Orange in 1688-9, L'Estrange lost his post as licenser, and as a consequence came a reduction of state control over the press. During his reign up to 1702 there were no government prosecutions of newspaper publishers or printers. This new-found freedom, combined with improvements in postal services, gave the independent press a real impetus. In the 1690s up to twenty one newspapers were circulating weekly, many incorporating "Post" in their titles.

Readers' interests widened. Politics and religion were no longer everyone's cup of tea or, rather, coffee for it was in these years that the coffee house as a meeting place for exchanging merchandise and ideas came into its own. Newspapers provided stimulus for flagging conversations. Gossip and entertainment became accepted and then demanded. Scandal sheets such as the *London Spy* (1698-1700) and the *Weekly Comedy; or, The Humours of a Coffee-House* (1707-1708) both edited by Edward Ward, proliferated. The *Athenian Mercury* (1690-1697)

Opposite:
MERCURIUS CIVICUS
No. 11
August 3-11, 1643
(180 x 135mm)
Note the 'headlines' top left of the first page. This Royalist newsbook was one of the first to incorporate 'Intelligencer' in its title.

33

The Man in the Moon,

Difcovering a World of

KNAVERY

Vnder the

SUNNE;

Both in the *Parliament* , the *Councell of State*, the *Army*, the *City*
and the COUNTRY.

With *Intelligence* from all Parts of *England*, *Scotland*,
and *IRELAND*.

Die Lunæ, From *June* 25. to *Wednefday*, *June* 27. 1649.

The *Caufe* again goes to the *worft*,
    which makes *Noll* fret and fwear
Sure *Brethren*, fure we are accurft,
    and then they tear their haire.

We know not what to fay nor do
    fince *Scots* do prove unkind,
But now we fhall to *Ireland* go
    when that the *Devil's* blind.

What fhall we do cryes *Martyn* then
    our *Members* do decreafe ,
Unlefs we have more *Money* and *Men*,
    we nere mult look for Peace.

Then in comes *Poppum* to the reft,
    and cryes out for more *Ships*,
Cromwel Inftructs which way is beft
    then to the *Citty trips*.

Were ever poor States put to fuch pittiful fhifts before ?
fure Deans and Chapters Lands are bewitch'd, they'd off
better elfe; new Difcoveries and the Revenue of the late King,
with all their Affeffements, Taxes, &c. will not do the feate :
          L   We

was an early question-and-answer paper copied by the *Ladies' Mercury* of 1693. The latter dealt only with:

> Questions of Love &c. . . . we promise they shall be weekly answered with all the zeal and softness becoming the sex; We likewise desire we may not be troubled with other Questions relating to Learning, Religion, &c, we resolving not to infringe on the Athenians.

The abolition of the licensing laws in word as well as deed in 1695 had another effect; finally to destroy the written newsletters which were still being produced until that year because domestic intelligence could legally be circulated in no other way. One printed newsletter maintained the tradition. *Dawks's News-Letter* started in 1696 and continued for twenty years. It was set in a special script typeface to emulate the written, individual quality of its predecessors.

> This letter will be done upon good writing paper, and blank space left that any gentleman may write his own private business. It does undoubtedly exceed the best of the written news, contains double the quantity, with abundance more ease and pleasure and will be useful to improve the younger sort in writing in a curious hand.

The hub of the Press in the seventeenth century was the hub of the country — London — but the history of the provincial press began well before 1700. *The Scots Scout's Discoveries* (1642), the *Scots Dove* (1643) and several other newsbooks were all published from London during the Civil War, though both camps carried travelling presses to produce newsbooks wherever they happened to be. The first genuine Scottish journal was *Mercurius Caledonius*, a weekly published in Edinburgh from December 1660 to March 1661. In 1688 there were no native-printed Scottish papers; the *Edinburgh Gazette* was first

Opposite:
THE MAN IN THE MOON
No. 18
June 26-27, 1649
(176 x 120mm)
'Die Lunae': Civil War satire
'Discovering a World of Knavery Under the Sunne'.

Overleaf:
THE PUBLICK INTELLIGENCER
No. 212
January 16-23, 1660
(232 x 180mm)
Marchamont Nedham produced Mercurius Politicus *(1650-1660) and The* Public Intelligencer *(1655-1660) as Cromwell's official newsbooks while independent publications were restricted.*

STRANGE NEWS FROM TOWER-DITCH
October 24, 1664
(180 x 130mm)
An unusual but rather sensational newsbook published after the return of Charles II, licensed to be printed by Roger L'Estrange, Surveyor of the Press.

Numb. 212.

THE
Publick Intelligencer

Communicating the Chief Occurrences

AND
PROCEEDINGS

WITHIN
The Dominions of *England*, *Scotland*, and I R E L A N D.

Together with an Account of Affairs from feveral Parts of *E V R O P E*.

Publifhed by Order of Parliament.

From Monday *January* 16. *to* Monday *January* 23. 1660.

From Edenburgh, Jan. 10.

Since the advance of my Lord General *Monck*, we have all things continue here in a calm and contented pofture; indeed by his magnanimity and prudence, he hath gained a great command over the affections of this people; fo that he hath rendred them very ferviceable to the intereft of the Commonwealth, and no ftirs need be feared here in his abfence, becaufe his enterprife for reftauration of the Parliament is very much approved by them, and divers of the Nobility and Gentry did

11 G   nos

36

STRANGE

N E VV S

FROM

Tovver-Ditch :

Being a Perfect Relation of the vaft
Quantity of F I S H taken there on Fryday the 20th.
of this inftant *October*.

With the ftrange manner of their coming in, in fuch abundance,
and how fome of them dyed and Stunk as foon as they
were handled , others were very fweet, and
eaten without any Ill Effects.

AS ALSO

The moft probable Conjectures of Intelligent perfons concerning
the Caufe or Reafon of this wonderful Accident.

This may be Printed , *October* 24. *Roger L'Eftrange.*

Printed for *P. Brooksby* in *Weft-Smith's-field.*

THE
NEWES,
PUBLISHED
For Satisfaction and Information
OF THE
PEOPLE.

With PRIVILEGE.

Thursday, March 17. 1663.

Hull, March 12.

Pon the *9th* of this *Instant*, was brought from *Lincoln* a Prisoner; by an *Ensigne* of the *Trayn-Band*, who was known to be a *Northumberland-man*, and had been observed to travel That Country divers times back and forward under several Names, Upon the 10*th Instant* he was carryed to *Beverly* to be Examined, and is now sent to *York-Castle* by order of the *Deputy-Lieutenants.* He appears to be a Person better qualifyed then ordinary for such an Employment; but we expect ere long to hear further concerning him,

Z   *Hague,*

38

Opposite: THE NEWES
No. 22
March 17, 1663
(250 x 165mm)
An early number of Roger
L'Estrange's Thursday
'supplement' to the
Intelligencer, *published on*
Mondays.

Above: THE LONDON GAZETTE
February 25, 1685 (300 x 185mm)
First published as the Oxford Gazette *in 1665 while the Royal Court was in exile there during*
the Great Plague in London, The London Gazette *was the first newspaper to have the look and*
feel of a newspaper in the modern sense of the word.

Mercurius Publicus,

COMPRISING

The Sum of all Affairs now in agitation
in *England*, *Scotland*, and *Ireland*,

Together with

FORRAIN INTELLIGENCE;

For Information of the People, and to
prevent false News

Published by Authority.

From Thursday *Novem.* 6. *to* Thursday *Novem.* 13. 1662.

Dover Novemb. 4. 1662.

HEre was a young man brought ashoar strangely
preserved; for on Saturday night about eight
a clock it being dark, two Dutch Ships met a-
bout the Dungel Nests, 20 miles from *Dover*,
& there fell foul upon one another, in so much
that one in which he was split to peices. The young man
betwixt sleeping and waking, when the Ship was sinking
caught hold of a short plank, and lived in the Sea before he
was taken up twelve or thirteen hours, till a boat come by

4 U   and

Right:
THE OBSERVATOR,
No. 81
June 16, 1684
(384 x 215mm)
Founded by Roger L'Estrange in 1681, The Observator discussed the news in somewhat cryptic dialogues here Titus Oates, fabricator of the 'Popish Plot'.

Left:
MERCURIUS PUBLICUS
No. 45
November 6-13, 1662
(210 x 154mm)
Produced by the Royalist newswriter, Henry Muddiman, after the restoration of the Monarchy in 1660. Like his predecessor Marchamont Nedham, Muddiman enjoyed a monopoly for reporting the news.

published in 1699. Three newspapers are reputed to have emanated from Dublin before the turn of the century: the *News Letter* (1685), *Dublin Intelligence* (1690-1694) and the *Dublin Gazette* (1689). Two English local papers claim to date from the 1690s: *Berrow's Worcester Journal* and the *Stamford Mercury*, but as no copies still exist, and the claims are based on local history, newspaper historians now seem to agree they both date from about 1710, leaving the *Norwich Post* 1701 as the earliest English provincial paper on the basis of backtracking from extant numbered issues of later years.

A certain Thomas Jones is said to have started publishing a monthly newspaper in the Welsh language at Shrewsbury in December 1690. The venture was unsuccessful and no issues of the publication have survived.

In the New World, only one issue of Benjamin Harris' *Publick Occurrences, Both Forreign and Domestick* appeared in 1690, in Boston, before it was suppressed by the Government of Massachusetts. A very short run indeed for America's first newspaper.

Right:
THE ATHENIAN
MERCURY
No. 17
April 19, 1691
(318 x 190mm)
An early question-and-answer paper, more information than news. In this issue answers are given on the ability of fleas to suck, bite or sting, and the proprietors honourably fail to endorse a cure for sword wounds 'without any plaister or any sort of application'.

Opposite:
DAWKS'S NEWS-LETTER
August 3, 1699
Set in a script typeface to imitate the earlier handwritten news-letters.

Numb. 17.

The Athenian Mercury:

Tuesday, *April* 19. 1691.

DAWKS's News-Letter.

Sr London

August 3. 699.

Last night we received an Holland Mail, with some of these particulars following.

Lemberg, July 11. The Baffa Bafigi, Treasurer General to the Grand Seignior, arrived at Caminieck on the 6th. instant, and gave Orders to the Governour to prepare to March out with his Garrison, and evacuate that Fortress to the Poles; whereupon the Turks have already begun to pack up their Baggage. The Hospodar of Walachia is also arrived upon the Frontiers, and is laying a Bridge over the Dniester, for the more convenient carrying of the Baggage. The Field Marshal of the Crown has sent to acquaint the King herewith.

Warsaw, July 18. The Diet is now like to have a good Issue, the King having Declared that he will maintain the Liberties of the People; that his Saxon Troops were all on their March homewards; That he will keep no Regiments by his Person, but only a Guard of 1200 Men at his own Charge, all of them Poles and Lithuanians: That if the Saxons do not March out of the Kingdom within the time limited, or return again on any Pretence whatsoever, without consent of the Republick, it shall be lawful for the Nobility to Assemble on Horseback without his Order, and Treat them as Publick Enemies. And in return hereof the Diet have obliged themselves to secure his Majesties Person with their utmost Power; that they will Severely Punish all that Act or but Speak against him: That all Libels against him shall be Burnt by the Hand of the Hangman: and the Authors of them serv'd in the same manner, if they can be apprehended. His Majesty will hold a Diet in Saxony in September; and its said he will bring his Queen hither with him when he returns.

Hamburg, August 4. Dr. Heiser, the Minister having Printed his Latin Oration upon the Marriage of the King of the Romans, on Cloth of Silver and Gold, and edg'd every Leaf of it with Point of Venice, which altogether cost this City 500 Crowns, he sent the same to the Emperor and King of the Romans, who have thereupon made the Doctor a Palsgrave, and given him his Patent free.

Hague, August 8. They write from Nieuerheusen in the County of Benthem, that 300 Neuburgers came to put the Countrey under Military Execution, for not submitting to the Popish Count; but that a Body of Dutch Soldiers advancing, who were sent by the States to support the Protestant Count, put the Neuburgers to flight, having kill'd a Lieutenant and wounded three others. Letters from Hungary say, that General Nehm, who was impower'd to be present at adjusting the Frontiers, falling into some Difference with the Bassa of Temeswaer, struck him Dead from his Horse; whereupon some other Turkish Officers taking up the Quarrel, there were 30 or 40 Men Killed on both sides; however the Commissioners went on with adjusting the Frontiers. Admiral Almer with his Squadron is Sail'd from Messina to Leghorn: The French Gallies shunn'd meeting him, because they knew he would oblige them to Strike. A Million of Crowns has been collected at Rome by way of Alms, for the Irish Papists as is given out. The refreshing Rains we have had of late, have in some manner dissipated the Fevers which raged in this Country, especially at Amsterdam, where People suffered

very

43

(Numb. 1.)

The Old Post=Master.

WITH THE

Occurrences of GREAT BRITTAIN and IRELAND, and from Foreign Parts; Collected and Published.

From **Saturday** *June* the 20th. to **Tuesday** *June* the 23th. 1696.

THIS Paper is intended constantly to be Published Three Days in the Week, viz. Tuesdays, Thursdays and Saturdays; and to contain only matters of Fact, without Reflections on Persons or Things: As also such other matters as will be found Useful for the Trading part of Mankind, as well Merchants as Mechanicks, &c. So many News Papers (as so called) are daily Published, that it would seem needless to trouble the World with more: ; but the difference of this Paper from those others Published, is with all modesty submitted to the judgment of every Judicious and Impartial Reader.

THe Advices from His Majesty's Camp, by the Holland Mail, which came in on Saturday, being in the Gazett and other Prints, I shall only add as follows, viz.

Paris June 21. We are extreamly surprized here, to hear of no action from any place, which makes News very bare; all our attention is on the side of Piedmont, being very impatient to see the issue of all our Negotiations with the Duke of Savoy: Couriers pass and repass the Mountains continually, and that which makes us the more uneasie, is to know how the Affair will be managed on that side, it, by reason of the Numerous Army that is kept there with so vast Expences and Charges, and great scarcity of Provisions, which cannot be sent to M. de Catinat's Camp without excessive Costs; but it was absolutely necessary to be Superiour in Force, to the Duke of Savoy, to Intimidate him, and to oblige him to come to a composition, and in that case, to turn with those Troops the Spaniards and Germans out of his Dominions, which was the only obstacle look'd upon at Court, that could hinder His Royal Highness from accepting the Advantageous Proposals which would be offered him for a Separate Peace.— The last Letters from the Army are of the 16th, but bring no News; they say only, that M. de Catinat, before he enters upon action, stays for an answer from the Duke of Savoy, about the pressing Solicitations made him from the King and the Pope. His Majesty sent an Express yesterday with his last Resolutions, at the instances of the Duke of Orleans, and gives that Prince time, till the end of this month to declare himself; and if he continues to reject the Kings orders, the M. de Catinat will go on, either to Bombard Turin, or to ruine the Plain, which he can reduce to such a Deplorable Condition, that the damage will not be made good in 30 years; which would be the utter ruine of Piedmont; the more, by reason that its chief Commerce consists in Silk, and that the Plain is full of Mulberry-Trees; a few days will make us wise, and learn its destiny: The mean while they write from Turin of the 12th, that M. de Catinat observes at present a very strict discipline in his Army, and does not tolerate the least vexation, though the Scarcity of Provisions begins a new in his Camp; we cannot imagine the reason of it, they pretend that he stays for his Artillery; but we are perswaded that such a General as M. de Catinat, would cause his orders to be better observed than so, if there were not some very important reasons that hindred it hitherto, which are unknown to us: They that come from Court assure, that 'tis discoursed there, that all the Articles of Composition between His Majesty and the Duke of Savoy, are agreed on by his Royal Highness, that there remains no other difficulty, than to make good the damage sustained by that Prince, which will be easily compised by the Pope's means, who labours hard to procure a Peace to Italy. An Express is arrived from Brest, dispatched by M. de Chateau Renaud, to know his Majesty's last resolution concerning the Squadron of 12 Men of War, which he is to command; they say at Court, that he is designed for Cruising on the Irish Coast, to Sail thence for Cape Finisterre, to pass the Streights, and to joyn the Mediterranean Men of War and Galleys that are arming with a design to besieg Barcelona by Sea, whilst the Duke de Vendome shall Attack it by Land; the great quantity of Ammunition and Provision that are laying up in Provence, together with the Detachments that are to be sent from Catinat's Army, after his Expedition in Piedmont, for Catalonia; confirm the opinion of the Sieg of that Important Place, after the great heats are over. 'Tis said that the Squadron of M. Ducasse is gone for the East-Indies; and that of Cape du Gennes, to cruise on the English and Dutch Coasts: and tho' some think that all our Naval Forces will act in several Squadrons; yet some are of opinion, that the Grand Fleet will put to Sea in August next, and that all the Privateers are to be called in, and ordered to come in Port by the end of July, in order to make use of their Equipages, as occasion shall require.

We have advice from Stockholm, that several Conferences have been held there with Count d' Avaux, about Peace, of which the King of Swedeland would fain be the only Mediator; and that the same might be Negociated in that Place ; but that the said Count d' Avaux has declared, the King his Master not to be of that opinion ; and that it will be convenient to regulate matters with England and the States of Holland, as to the quality King William must be treated with, before he enters upon any Negotiation.

Its wrote from Cologne, that the French have burnt Treves; but we hope it will need a confirmation.

Francfort June the 20th. The Allies on the upper Rhine have now finished their Line, which, when their Army passes that River, is to be guarded by 12 or 15000 of the Militia, to secure the Countrey for Wortemberg from a French Invasion. The French continue to desert in great numbers, and their Army is still in the fear

44

1700-1790
THE DAILY PAPER: FIGHT FOR PRESS FREEDOM

The *Post Boy* of 1695, a thrice-weekly, had for four days tried to go daily, but the experiment was not successful. The first daily paper to survive was the *Daily Courant*, launched on 11 March 1702, three days after Queen Anne ascended the throne, and expired only in 1735 when it merged with the *Daily Gazetteer*. It was not until the *Daily Oracle* of 1715 that it had competition from another daily. The format was like the *London Gazette*, but printed on only one side. The first printer explained that he did this "to save the Publick at least half the Impertinences of ordinary newspapers", logic that might have persuaded him to sell just blank sheets. Its subject matter was, however nothing but news, "supposing other people to have sense enough to make reflections for themselves", a revolutionary principle.

The first appearance of the word "evening" in a title came with the *Evening Post* of 1706, a thrice-weekly. In the provinces, activity greatly increased. The *Edinburgh Courant* of 1705 followed in the footsteps of the *Edinburgh Gazette*. Several newspapers emanated from Norwich before 1715: the *Postman* (1706) — price "a penny, but a halfpenny not refused", the *Norwich Courant* (1714), the *Norwich Gazette* (1706) — the earliest first issue to have survived. Other centres of the press were Exeter with the *Post-Boy* (1709) and *Samuel Farley's Exeter Post Man* (1704); Bristol — the *Post Boy* (1704); Newcastle — *Gazette* (1710) and *Courant* (1711); Northampton — *Mercury* (1720) and *Journal* (1722). By 1725 York, Yarmouth, Leeds, Gloucester, Liverpool were among several provincial towns with their own newspapers.

The main concern of these locals was to find enough material to fill the pages. Typically, they resorted to reprinting foreign reports, as the first corantos had done a century earlier. Parliament still could not be reported. At the same time, the papers aimed to be as interesting as possible to

Opposite:
THE OLD POST-MASTER
No. 1
June 20-23, 1696
(380 x 220mm)

45

Right:
THE TATLER
No. 59
August 23-25, 1709
(340 x 240mm)
With absolutely no pretence of objectivity, the Tatler *promised to instruct its readers 'what to think'; founded by Sir Richard Steele who, as Isaac Bickerstaff wrote 188 of the 271 issues.*

Opposite:
THE EVENING POST
No. 718
March 13-16, 1714
(263 x 210mm)
The first newspaper to include 'evening' in its title; founded in 1706 as a thrice-weekly.

The TATLER.

Numb. 59

By Isaac Bickerstaff Esq;

Quicquid agunt Homines nostri Farrago Libelli.

From *Tuesday August* 23. to *Thursday August* 25. 1709.

The Evening Poſt.

Numb. 718.

From Saturday March 13. to Tueſday March 16. 1714

Since our laſt arriv'd One Mail from France.

From the Paris A-la-main.
Paris, March 21.

E have receiv'd Letters directly from Conſtantinople, of the 1ſt of February, which confirm the Defeat of the Baſhaws, who rebell'd in Aſia ; ſo that the Troops, which had been order'd thither, are countermanded. 'Tis added, That they continu'd their Levies and other military Preparations, particularly on the Side of Salonica ; and that they were working with great Application in other Ports of the Archipelago, to equip a Fleet, which is to be commanded by the Captain Baſhaw: The ſaid Fleet conſiſts of 32 Sultana's, 20 Gallies, and as many Galeaſſes, and is to ſail in the Month of May : 'Twas not known for what Expedition ; but 'twas conjectur'd it might be in Favour of his Swediſh Majeſty and King Staniſlaus, for whom the Grand Signior appears to intereſt himſelf ſtill.

We are adviſ'd from Straſburg, the 10th, and from Nancy, the 13th, that the two Generals parted the 7th, at Raſtad, Prince Eugene for Vienna, by the Way of Auſburg, and Marſhal Villars for Straſburg, where he ſtay'd from the 8th to the 10th. Two Days after he arriv'd at the Caſtle of Salus, in Franche Conte, where he found the Duke of Lorrain expecting him : The Duke entertain'd him with great Magnificence ; and after having held a long Conference, they parted the 13th, the Duke for Ludeville, and the Marſhal for Paris. 'Tis not queſtion'd, that this Interview related to the Pretenſions of his Royal Highneſs to the Dutchy of Mantua and the Montferrat, which the Marſhal, by the King's Order, had inſiſted on ſtrenuouſly at Raſtad ; and 'tis ſaid he has obtain'd a ſatisfactory Equivalent for the ſaid Pretenſions. Whether this be ſo or not, the Duke of Lorrain continues his Levies in his Dominions, but not out of them, for a ſecret Expedition.

The Chevalier de St. George has been viſited, for ſome Days, at Bar-le Duc, by the Prince and Princeſs of Vaudemont, who are ſince gone back to Commercy. As ſoon as the Peace was ſign'd, the French and German Governors of the Frontier Places along the Rhine, receiv'd Order to cauſe Hoſtilities to ceaſe, till the Suſpenſion of Arms ſhould be proclaim'd.

Marſhal Villars was very graciouſly receiv'd by the King, who confer'd on his Son the Survivance of the Government of Provence ; and we are alſo inform'd, that the Marſhal has obtain'd his Majeſty's Pardon for Prince Eugene.

The Madrid Poſt is not yet arriv'd ; but we are adviſ'd, by Letters from Gironne, of the 6th Inſtant, that Count de Fiennes has ſent thither two Leaders of the Rebels, and that Don Vallejo has ſent ſome other Leaders to Solſona. All is quiet again in Catalonia, except

in the Luſanes, where are ſtill ſome Troops of Miquelets, which are Maſters of the Paſſages of the Mountains ; but the King's Troops continue to purſue them, in order to reſtore, on every Side, the Communication with the Army before Barcelona. Furthermore, the Marquis de Thouy having aſſembled near Lerida, 2000 Horſe and 40 Battalions, has ſent Detachments to Cardona, to reinforce the Blockade of that Caſtle. On the 25th paſt, the Marquis de Mari join'd the Squadron, which is ſtill at the Mouth of the Lobregat, with the Men of War, he equip'd at Genoa. At the ſame Time the King's Ships took two Pinks laden with Proviſions for the Rebels. On the other hand, the Revolters, by Favour of the Night, took from the Spaniards two Genoeſe Veſſels and five Tartanes belonging to Languedoc ; but they had been unloaded before they fell into the Enemy's Hands.

Rome, Feb. 17.
On Sunday laſt, arriv'd here ſeveral Coaches and Waggons, with Count Gallas's Family, which alighted at the Palace of Prince Odeſchalchi ; ſo that his Excellency is not far off. The Cardinal de Bouillon is ſhortly expected alſo from Florence, at which Court he has made ſome Stay.

Hamburg, March 16.
We are adviſ'd from Copenhagen, that Count Steinbock has obtain'd Permiſſion to go to Schonen, for the Recovery of his Health, and looking after ſome of his private Concerns ; but he has engag'd to meddle with no publick Affairs, and deſir'd an Officer may go along with him to have Eye-witneſs of his Conduct. The Papers found in Tonningen, when the Danes took that Place, have been examin'd in Council ; and it appears by Letters to M. Wolf, the late Governor, and other authentick Writings, that Tonningen was deliver'd to General Steinbock, by Order of the young Duke of Holſtein, and by Conſent of the Adminiſtrator. Letters from Poland confirm, that the Palatine of Kiow, Prince Wiſſnowiſki, and the Generals Smigielki and Criſpin have abandon'd the Party of Swedes, and are on their Way to Dreſden, to make their Submiſſion to King Auguſtus ; and as they were the chief Supporters of the Intereſt of Staniſlaus, 'tis believ'd the whole Republick will be ſoon reunited under the King of Poland's Obedience. That Prince continues in Saxony, and will not return to Warſaw, till he ſees the Succeſs of the Negotiations at Brunſwick, where the Congreſs is open'd ; tho' all the Miniſters, who are expected there, are not yet arriv'd. 'Tis adviſ'd from Poland, that the Turks continue their military Preparations ; and that the Tartars were making Diſpoſitions for an Invaſion, whereupon the Crown General has ſent Orders to the Poliſh Troops on the Frontiers, to ſtand upon their Guard, and written to General Janus, to have the Saxon Troops in Readineſs, that they may join the Forces of the Republick in Caſe of Neceſſity.

Hague,

THE DAILY COURANT
No. 4978
October 3, 1717
(350 x 180mm)
The first successful daily
published newspaper,
1702-1735.

Bbbbbbbbb   Numb. 4978

The Daily Courant.

Thursday, October 3. 1717.

Warfaw, September 17.

THEY have deliberated in the General Diet of the Palatinate of Mafovia, among other things, upon the Means of caufing the Ruffians to depart the Kingdom, according to the late Treaty, to which Purpofe, two Starofts were deputed to his Majefty, and to the Crown General. The Count de Viemond, at the fame time that he complain'd in the Emperor's Name, that Count Eberhall had been allow'd to pafs thro' Poland into Tranfilvania, and that feveral Polanders had pafs'd the Frontiers, and taken Service with the Turks, [the Anfwer to which we have already mention'd, namely, that the Crown General had taken all poffible Care to prevent it,] propos'd further, that Poland fhould take hold of the favourable Opportunity that prevents it fuff, and join their Forces to thofe of the Emperor, for the fooner and more effectually reducing to Reafon the common Enemy of the Chriftian Name ; To which his Majefty has anfwer'd, That his Excellency was not ignorant that the Crown of Poland was ftill engag'd in the War with Sweden, and confequently not in a Condition to take up Arms againft any other Enemy. But if his Imperial Majefty will concur, by his powerful Authority, to deliver the Crown of Poland from that Enemy, and to fecure the Repofe of the Republick of Poland on the Side of Sweden, his Majefty will then convoke the States of his Realm, and make ufe of all his Efforts, to induce them to turn their Arms, as he defires, againft the Common Enemy.

Berlin, Sept. 28. This Court has again received Letters from his Imperial Majefty, the like whereof have been fent to Hanover ; wherein his faid Majefty fignifies, that in Cafe Execution of the Imperial Decree againft the Duke of Mecklenburg be not fpeedily made, to the Satisfaction of his Imperial Majefty, he is pofitively refolved to caufe the Regiments that have not fuffered in the late Battle in Hungary to pafs into Silefia, and from thence to march into the Dutchy of Mecklenburg, in order to caufe them to put the faid Decree into Execution. Whereupon his Pruffian Majefty has fent Lieut. Col. Riewe to the Duke of Mecklenburg, to exhort him to accommodate Matters with his Nobility without Delay, and thereby give Satisfaction to the Emperor ; in Default whereof, His Majefty, in Conjunction with the Electoral Houfe of Hanover, will be obliged to put the Imperial Decree in Execution themfelves, not being willing to permit the Imperial Troops to pafs thro' their Dominions to do it.

Firft of the Houfe of Commons of Ireland.

Dublin, Sept. 22. Lieutenant General Hamilton Reported from the Committee appointed to attend his Grace the Lord Lieutenant with the Addrefs of this Houfe, in Favour of William Purefoy, Efq; That they had attended his Grace accordingly, and that his Grace was pleafed to fay, He would lay the fame before his Majefty in the beft Manner he could for the Advantage of Mr. Purefoy.

A Petition of the Provoft, Fellows, and Scholars of Trinity College near Dublin, fetting forth, That purfuant to an Addrefs of the Houfe of Commons in 1709, the Petitioners received 5000 l. and have faithfully and carefully laid it out towards erecting a Library, but that the faid Sum is not fufficient to finifh that Work : And declaring their Refolution to inftruct the Youth under their Care in Principles of Zeal and Affection to the Conftitution in Church and State, and of Duty and Loyalty to His Majefty King George, and His Royal Family, was prefented to the Houfe and read.

Refolved, Nem. Con. That this Houfe do addrefs his Grace the Lord Lieutenant, that he will lay before His Majefty the humble Defire of this Houfe, That His Majefty will be pleafed out of his Royal Bounty, to give to the Provoft, Fellows, and Scholars of Trinity College near Dublin, fuch Sum or Sums not exceeding 5000 l. as he fhall from time to time judge neceffary to be expended, towards finifhing the Library of the faid College.

Ordered, That fuch Members of this Houfe as are of His Majefty's moft Honourable Privy Council, do attend his Grace the Lord Lieutenant with the faid Addrefs, and lay the fame before his Grace.

Mr. Chancellour of the Exchequer Reported from the Committee appointed to take into Confideration the Petition of William Ormsby, Efq; That they had come to feveral Refolutions in the Matter to them referred, which he read in his Place, and after delivered at the Table, where the fame were again read, and are as follow.

Refolved, That it is the Opinion of this Committee, That the Petitioner hath fully proved the Allegations of his Petition.

Refolved, That it appears to this Committee, That the Petitioner's Father raifed a Troop of Horfe, and the Petitioner a Company of Foot, in the Year 1688, at their own Expence, for the Defence of the Proteftant Intereft and Liberties of their Country, and the Service of His late Majefty King William of Glorious Memory.

Refolved, That it appears to this Committee, that the Petitioner was forced to quit his Command in the Army, tho' willing and ready to ferve.

Refolved, That it is the Opinion of this Committee, That the Petitioner be recommended to his Grace the Lord Lieutenant, to be put upon the Eftablifhment for Half Pay as Major and Captain, and to continue thereon until provided for.

To which Refolutions the Queftion being feverally put, the Houfe did agree.

Ordered, That fuch Members of this Houfe as are of His Majefty's moft Honourable Privy Council, do attend his Grace the Lord Lieutenant with the faid Petition and Refolutions, and lay the fame before his Grace, to the End the Petitioner may be put upon the Eftablifhment for Half Pay as Major and Captain, and to continue thereon until provided for.

Martis, Sept. 24. Mr. Chancellor of the Exchequer Reported from the Committee appointed to attend his Grace the Lord Lieutenant with the Addrefs of this Houfe in Favour of Trinity-College near Dublin, That they had attended his Grace accordingly, and that thereupon his Grace was pleafed to return the Anfwer following.

I Will lay the Addrefs of the Houfe of Commons in Favour of the College before His Majefty, and I make no doubt but His Majefty will Comply therewith, in regard of the Duty and Zeal they have fhewn to His Royal Perfon and Government.

Mr. Parry Reported from the Committee appointed to attend his Grace the Lord Lieutenant with the Addrefs of this Houfe in Favour of Mr. Theobalds Jones, That they had attended his Grace accordingly, and that his Grace was pleafed to fay, That he would lay the fame before His Majefty in the beft and moft effectual Manner, according to the Defire of the Commons.

A Petition of Charles Northcote, Clerk, fetting forth, That this Houfe was pleafed the laft Seffion to Recommend him to the then Lords Juftices for fome Ecclefiaftical Preferment, as well for his Sufferings in the late War in this Kingdom, as for his conftant Zeal and Fidelity to His prefent Majefty and the Proteftant Succeffion in His Illuftrious Houfe, but that the Petitioner hath not received the Benefit of the faid Recommendation, and praying that this Houfe will renew the fame to his Grace the Lord Lieutenant, was prefented to the Houfe and Read.

Refolved, Nem. Con. That the Petitioner Mr. Charles Northcote, be Recommended to his Grace the Lord Lieutenant in the moft effectual Manner for fome Ecclefiaftical Dignity, as well for his Sufferings in the late War in this Kingdom, as for his conftant Zeal and Fidelity to His prefent Majefty and the Proteftant Succeffion in His Illuftrious Houfe.

Ordered, That the faid Recommendation be laid before his Grace by fuch Members of this Houfe as are of His Majefty's moft honourable Privy-Council.

The Order for the Day being Read.

Refolved, That this Houfe do on Friday next Refolve it felf into a Committee of the whole Houfe, to take into Confideration the Supply granted to His Majefty, and alfo his Grace the Lord Lieutenant's Speech.

London, October 3.

Late laft Night arriv'd a Mail from France. The Paris Gazette mentions the Accident at Barcelona, where the Magazine was blown up by Lightning ; and the News-Letter fays the Spanish Ambaffadour at Paris has receiv'd Letters from Marfeilles, with Advice that the Spaniards are Cannonading the City of Cagliari : But he does not mention the Date of thofe Letters. The further Particulars brought by this Mail, fhall be communicated in our next.

London, October 3.

Yefterday South Sea Stock was 115 3 qrs. to 112. Bank 147 3 qrs. to 148 one qr. India 195 3 qrs. to 197. African 19 one half.

prevent rivals starting up in their area. They mixed in with the foreign news, local news, abstracts of "all the papers of note", murders, fires, foreign intelligence, advertisements, but were often short of copy. The editor of the *British Spy or Derby Post-Man* wrote to his readers in 1728:

> When the Mails fail us and the people are inactive at home, when Great Folks are so ill-natur'd as neither to marry nor die nor beget children, we are upon the search for that scarce commodity called wit, which 'tis well known, is in these Days as hard to come at in any week (especially in Derby) as Intelligence.

The *Leicester Journal* got so hard up in 1752 that it began reprinting the Bible and reached the tenth chapter of Exodus before giving up this attempt at serialisation of the world's best-seller, perhaps in a misguided effort to emulate its success.

When the *Northampton Journal* started in July 1722 in some ways it must have been a godsend to the *Mercury* by then just over two year's old. No love was lost between them, but their battle for the limited number of readers in Northampton helped to fill the pages. The *Mercury* condemned the *Journal's* "new upstart Author who, bigoted in himself, and nurtur'd in his foolish opinions by others (has) lavishly thrown money away on a Press'. The Author was further described as a "noisy animal" with a "doating brain", a "thick and stupid Crannium", and the initial issue of the *Journal* dismissed as "his first parcel of bum-fodder".

If the country editors had nothing to say, there were others who did. Writers such as Daniel Defoe, Jonathan Swift, Joseph Addison and Richard Steele used the medium to carry vials of political venom and satire. Defoe edited and wrote most of the *Weekly Review* (1704-1713); its first numbers were written while Defoe was gaoled in Newgate. Jonathan Swift wrote for a Tory paper, the *Examiner* (1710-1714); Addison and Steele responded on the Whig side with a variety of papers: The *Whig Examiner* (1710), the *Medley* (1710-1712), the *Freeholder* (1715-1716), the *Guardian* (no links with its modern namesake) (1713), the *Englishman* (1714-1715), most famously, the thrice-weekly *Tatler* (1709-1711), and the *Spectator* (1711-1712). These "essay papers" were concerned as much with pushing a particular political viewpoint as reporting the news. Their philosophy can be summed up by the opening paragraph of the *Tatler* in its first issue, Tuesday, April 12, 1709.

> Tho' the other Papers which are publish'd for the Use of the good People of Englande have certainly very wholesome effects, and are laudable in their particular Kinds, they do not seem to come up to the main Design of such Narrations, which I humbly presume, should be principally intended for the Use of Politick Persons, who are so publick-spirited as to neglect their own Affairs to look into Transactions of State. Now these gentlemen, for the most Part, being Persons of strong Zeal and weak Intellects, It is both a Charitable and Necessary work to offer something, whereby such worthy and well-affected Members of the Commonwealth may be instructed, after their Reading, *what to think.*

Duty Stamp
Half penny
August 1712

The power of the press, and the sheer volume of publications, frightened the government into imposing a Stamp Duty on all papers and advertisements in August 1712, a halfpenny on half a sheet, a penny on a whole sheet (four pages). But a loophole in the Act allowed six pages to go untaxed. Defoe's *Review* ceased publication, but most papers did not go to the wall as Swift had predicted (duties were not strictly levied until 1725) but the higher cover

Volume 22. THE Numb. 1114.

Norwich Gazette.

From Saturday February 3, to Saturday February 10, 1728.

MONDAY, February 5. *On Saturday last arrived a Mail from Holland.*

Cadix, January 13.

E hear from Gibraltar, that the Troops of Spain are quitting the Camp with all Expedition. All the Silver brought hither from Vera Cruz, will be deliver'd to the Proprietors before the End of this Week ; and they will immediately after begin with the Cochineal, and the other Merchandizes. The King's Share amounts to about one Fourth, and the Silver is to be coined in the Mints.

Madrid, January 10. The King having been for some Days ill of a Fever at Pardo, is now much better, and 'tis hoped His Majesty will be soon rid of it. They write from Biscay, that Two new Men of War have been launched there.

Vienna, January 28. We are informed by Letters from Poland, That there are 3 several Factions in that Kingdom on Account of the Succession, one for the Electoral Prince of Saxony, another for Prince Sobieski, and the 3d and strongest for King Stanislaus. Some Advices from Constantinople say, That the Grand Seignior intends to send a solemn Ambassie hither, to make advantagious Proposals to the Emperor, that he may continue Neuter in Case of a Rupture betwixt the Ottoman Porte and Russia.

Cambray, January 31. An Express from Madrid has brought the agreeable News, That Spain not judging it proper to force the Allies of Hanover into a War, had granted all they asked, except 2 Points of small Importance ; so that the Ratification of the Preliminaries will immediately follow.

Hamburg, February 3. Letters from Poland say, That the Interview between the Kings of Poland and Prussia at Dresden, occasions much Umbrage among the Grandees of that Kingdom. Letters from Petersburg say, That the Duke of Liria was in Treaty for 12 Russian Men of War to be ready to enter into the King his Master's Service.

Cologn, February 6. Yesterday passed thro' here a Courier from the Hague for Vienna, with the *Ultimatum* of the King of Spain, concerning the Ratification of the Preliminaries.

Paris, January 31. A Person was lately apprehended at Court, who pretended to be an Envoy from the Holy Ghost, and presented a Paper to His Majesty, exhorting him to make War upon the Hereticks and Infidels. They write from Picardy, that there's a vast Resort of People to Pons, to see a Giri there, who, though but 12 Years of Age, is 6 Foot high, and is still growing.

Hague, February 10. The Accommodation of the Differences between Great Britain and Spain, is a done Thing ; Mr. Finch the English Minister having declared in a Conference held with the Marquis of Fenelon, and their High Mightinesses Deputies for Foreign Affairs, that the King his Master had accepted of the *Ultimatum* of the King of Spain, which was communicated to him by the Court of France. This *Ultimatum* is rather for Form, than any Thing else ; for it contains nothing in it that can change or deviate from the Preliminary Articles, except a few Additions concerning the Decision of the Pretensions and Counter-Pretensions of those 2 Powers, which are to be discussed in the Congress of Cambray. And thus the Restitution of the Ship Prince Frederick is not limited to any Time.

Shields, January 24. On the 19th Instant a Pink belonging to Yarmouth, one Sunderland Master, was lost by a Storm of Wind, but all the Crew were saved.

London, February 3. On Wednesday was held at the South Sea House a General Court of the said Company, for the Consideration of what Dividend should be made ; the Questions for 1 half, 1 1 4th, and 1 1 8th were severally put, but rejected by a great Majority. Mr. Tully moved for 1 half, and Mr. Lade for making no Dividend at all, but the Majority appeared to be most inclined to 1 per Cent ; to which it was objected that it would be absurd, this being the same Court which had rejected it : On which a Motion was made for putting the Question a 1 4th a second Time, which was carried and agreed on accordingly, the Warrants to bear Date February 1, and to be paid the 20th.

WYE's Letter to Day has the 5 following Paragraphs, viz. Yesterday the House of Commons waited on His Majesty at St. James's with their Address, wherein they humbly represented, amongst other Things, their Sense of the unwearied and uninterrupted Care with which His Majesty has laboured to put an End, and restore the Tranquility of Europe ; as also the Firmness His Majesty has shewn in absolutely refusing to admit of any Explanation of the Preliminaries, derogatory to the Honour or prejudicial to the Interest of the Nation : That since this Stand, which His Majesty in Justice to his People thought fit to make, has not broke off the Accommodation, but retarded it to our Advantage, they beg Leave to congratulate His Majesty upon the near Prospect of Success in his Negotiations ; but in Case His Majesty's Expectations, of seeing the Publick Peace and Tranquil ity ... should still be disappointed, that your People ... continue in that Uncertainty in which the Policy ... endeavour to keep us, they will most effectually ... Majesty to do himself Right, and to assert and ...

THE NORWICH GAZETTE, No. 1114, February 3-10, 1718 (300 x 220mm).

A
REVIEW
OF THE
STATE
OF THE
BRITISH NATION.

𝕾𝖆𝖙𝖚𝖗𝖉𝖆𝖞, February 18. 1710.

IT is not often that I have taken upon me to talk in the first Person to the High Gentlemen, they are dangerous Folks to be so free with, as I find needful ; but who can help speaking to them, their Behaviour at this Time is so particular and remarkable, who' can avoid admonishing them a little ?

At the first Questioning Dr. *Sacheverell* before the *House* of *Commons*, the Insolence and Fury of the Party was extravagantly great, the Doctrine preach'd by *Sacheverell* was nothing but Truth, and the whole Nation would stand by it, and the *House* dar'd not to go on with it—— And indeed they acted in all Company, as if their Party was too considerable in *England* to be at-tack'd, even by the *House* of *Commons*—— But this first Heat began too cool, when they found the *House* in earnest ; that they impeach'd the *Doctor*, refus'd him Bail, and prepar'd their Articles——

As soon as these Articles were exhibited, and the *Doctor* had Time given to make his Answer, the *Houses* going on upon other Business——The Gentlemen spread about a new Fiction of their own; *Viz.* That the *House* had only made a Bluster, that it was a Heat and would cool again, that the moderate Gentlemen of the Church of *England* began to repent falling upon the Church with such Fury, that they saw it only gratify'd the Phanaticks, and encourag'd the Enemies of the Church ; and that they saw,

Dr.

The SCOURGE.

A Bishop must be blameless as the Steward of God, not Self willed, for there are many Unruly and Vain Talkers, whose Mouths must be stopped. Epist. to Titus, Ch. i. 7, 10, 11.

MONDAY *June* 3. 1717.

THE *Apostolical* Institution of *Episcopacy* has been so *unusually* received in the *English* Nation, that it must be strangely disagreeable to hear the Character of a *Bishop* become the Scorn and Ridicule of a whole Kingdom, and made the subject of the most Vulgar and Licentious Conversation. But more shocking is the Reflection when a Prelate has so far *Abdicated* the Dignity of his Sacred Office, as to expose his Integrity to the universal Odium of Mankind, to give up the Rights of his Holy Function, and, to all appearance, approve himself an Apostate to his own Orders.

The Lowest Insults of Communion have basely asserted the Honour of Religion and of our Ecclesiastical Establishment; and his Lordship of *Bangor*, by the same, I suppose is convinced how singular he is in his Opinions, and that it is not the general Belief of the Clergy of *England* that our *Liturgy* is no more than *Superstitious Toys*, our Rubrick a *Rule of Art*; and that Repentance and a Godly Sorrow depend only upon *Custom* or *Constitution*, and are unnecessary *Terms of our Acceptance with God*. For my own Part, I humbly hope his Lordship will permit me without Censure, to join in the Common Service of our Church, till he is pleased to fulfil his Promise, and oblige us with a *New Form of Prayer* of his own composing, which his Lordship, because I presume our *Established* Form is Criminal and Deficient, imagines he has now a just Occasion to reckon the World withal. I humbly beg likewise that notwithstanding his Lordship has told me, that no Man is either more or less sensible of his Sins for Prayer or our forbidding Texts, I may, if it should please God to afflict me with any Dangerous Sickness, be allowed to have the Office for the *Visitation of the Sick* read to me, wherein the Priest implores the Divine Mercy to consider my Contrition and accept my Tears; and this Favour I have some

Assurance of, because his Lordship has been pleased to confess that *he endeavours to interpret the Doctrines of Christ, without the Thoughts that all who hear him are indispensably obliged to receive his Interpretation*.

In a late Reign I find several Discourses published under the Titles of *The Reasonableness of Conformity to the Church of England*; *A Persuasive to Lay-Conformity*; *A Defence of Episcopal Ordination*, and a *Reply to Mr.* Calamy, a Dissenting Teacher, by Benjamin *Hoadly*, M.A. Rector of St. *Peters Poor*; and I have been often told, that this Divine was some time ago advanc'd to the See of *Bangor*, and preached before the King at St. *James*'s upon the 43d of *March*; but I have been reason to believe, that my Information was a Mistake, and that his present Lordship of *Bangor*, and the late Rector of St. *Peters* are not the SAME; their Schemes of Religion and Government are so widely distant, that if I walk with the Instructions of Mr. *Hoadly* I may, if I please, by a tolerable good Subject, and be persuaded that it is my Duty to conform to the Discipline and Doctrines of the Church, but if I am directed by his Lordship, I may lawfully think myself free from all Obedience to my Superiors. I must believe the Church of Christ to be a State of Anarchy and Confusion, that every Man is left to do what is right in his own Eyes, and I may absolutely deny the Supremacy of my Sovereign. It must be excusable therefore when I appear in Vindication of Honest Mr. *Hoadly*, and reform his Character from that Infamy and Reproach, that have fallen upon the Principles of the Bishop. And to let this Matter in the clearest Light, I shall fairly produce a short Specimen in their own Words, and refer it to the Arbitration of all reasonable Men, whether it is possible that the same Person could ever be so lost to his Memory and Religion, as to be guilty of such contrary Positions, such unfaithful and scandalous Contradictions.

Tur

Above: THE SCOURGE, No. XVIII, June 3, 1717 (300 x 190mm), edited by T. Lewis.

Opposite: A REVIEW OF THE STATE OF THE BRITISH NATION, No. 136, February 18, 1710, known as the 'Weekly Review', edited and largely written by Daniel Defoe.

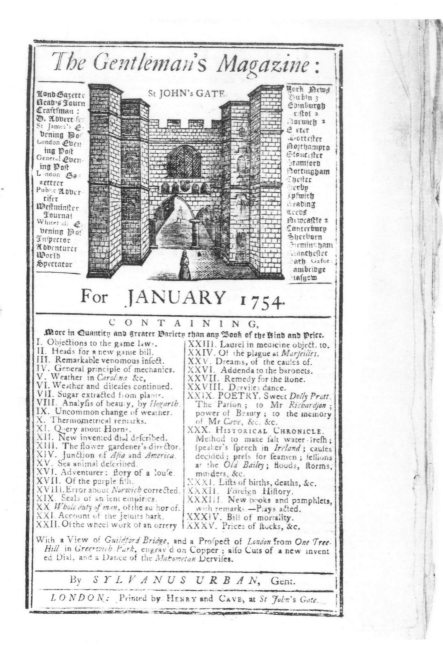

The Gentleman's Magazine:

St JOHN's GATE.

Lond Gazette
Read's Journ
Craftsman:
D. Advertiser
St James's Evening Post
London Evening Post
General Evening Post
London Gazetteer
Public Advertiser
Westminster Journal
Whitehall Evening Post
Inspector
Adventurer
World
Spectator

York News
Dublin 3
Edinburgh
Bristol 2
Norwich 2
Exeter
Worcester
Northampto
Gloucester
Stamford
Nottingham
Chester
Derby
Ipswich
Reading
Leeds
Newcastle 2
Canterbury
Sherborn
Birmingham
Manchester
Bath Oxfor
Cambridge
Glasgow

For JANUARY 1754.

CONTAINING,

More in Quantity and greater Variety than any Book of the Kind and Price.

I. Objections to the game laws.
II. Heads for a new game bill.
III. Remarkable venomous insect.
IV. General principle of mechanics.
V. Weather in *Carolina* &c,
VI. Weather and diseases continued.
VII. Sugar extracted from plants.
VIII. Analysis of beauty, by *Hogarth*.
IX. Uncommon change of weather.
X. Thermometrical remarks.
XI. Query about Horns.
XII. New invented dial described.
XIII. The flower gardener's director.
XIV. Junction of *Asia* and *America*.
XV. Sea animal described.
XVI. Adventurer: story of a louse.
XVII. Of the purple fish.
XVIII. Error about *Norwich* corrected.
XIX. Seals of antient empirics.
XX. *Whole duty of man*, of the author of.
XXI. Account of the Jesuits bark.
XXII. Of the wheel work of an orrery

XXIII. Laurel in medicine object. to.
XXIV. Of the plague at *Marseilles*.
XXV. Dreams, of the causes of.
XXVI. Addenda to the baronets.
XXVII. Remedy for the stone.
XXVIII. Dervises dance.
XXIX. POETRY. Sweet *Dolly Pratt*.
The Parson; to Mr *Richardson*;
power of Beauty; to the memory
of Mr *Cave*, &c. &c.
XXX. HISTORICAL CHRONICLE.
Method to make salt water fresh;
speaker's speech in *Ireland*; causes
decided; press for seamen; sessions
at the *Old Bailey*; floods, storms,
murders, &c.
XXXI. Lists of births, deaths, &c.
XXXII. Foreign History.
XXXIII. New books and pamphlets,
with remarks.—Plays acted.
XXXIV. Bill of mortality.
XXXV. Prices of stocks, &c.

With a View of *Guildford Bridge*, and a Prospect of *London* from *One Tree Hill* in *Greenwich Park*, engrav'd on Copper; also Cuts of a new invented Dial, and a Dance of the *Mahometan* Dervises.

By *SYLVANUS URBAN*, Gent.

LONDON: Printed by HENRY and CAVE, at *St John's Gate*.

54

Opposite:
THE GENTLEMAN'S
MAGAZINE
January, 1754
(230 x 148mm)

A blend of news, entertainment
and information; the most
successful of the
eighteenth-century news
magazines.

Duty Stamp
One penny
August 1712

price did restrict sales. To fill an untaxed six pages, the essayists were given more space to 'editorialise' and it is from about this time that the histories of the news-papers and the more discursive essay-papers or magazines start to diverge.

The main newspapers of the 1720s and 1730s were the *Craftsman* (1726-1747?), *Daily Courant* (1702-1735), *Daily Gazetteer* (1735-1748), *British Journal* (1722-1731?), *London Journal* (1719-1744), *Old Whig* (1735-1738?), *Free Briton* (1729-1735) and the *Grub Street Journal* (1730-1737), all fighting one another. The *Daily Advertiser* (1730-1807) marked a change in the commercial side of the press — the printer-publisher began to give way to the proprietor who could develop the paper as a 'business'. Income from the printing of paid advertisements also became a more significant factor in the commercial success of that business.

Political disputes between Whigs and Tories were of major interest to readers, but reporting them was difficult in the extreme. Parliament confirmed again in 1722 the prohibition of reporting its affairs.

The *Gentleman's Magazine,* a monthly founded by Edward Cave in 1731, overcame this restriction by calling the Parliament of Britain, in its 1736 pages, the Senate of Great Lilliput. The pen of Samuel Johnson turned Dukes into "Nardacs", Lords became "Hurgoes" and the Commons, "Clinabs". Names were similarly thinly disguised. The *Gentleman's* (and the *London) Magazine* were reprimanded in 1747, but Cave continued the practice again in 1752.

Not until the 1760s was the ban effectively opposed rather than evaded by subtlety. John Wilkes MP, in his paper the *North Briton* (1762-1763), established to counter Tobias Smolletts's reactionary *The Briton* (1762-1763), made constant attacks on George III and the Tory Government. In 1763, after "Number 45", Wilkes and all the others working on the paper

Whitehall Evening-Poſt.

From Saturday, March 2. to Tueſday, March 5. 1722-23.

From the Amſterdam Gazette in French.

Paris, March 1.

WE hear from Martinico, that the Governour of that Place is preparing to oppoſe the taking Poſſeſſion of St. Lucia by the Engliſh, which Iſland, tho' diſtant only 7 Miles from Martinico, is not inhabited; this Court not having thought it proper to ſeize the ſame leaſt it ſhould have given ſome Jealouſy to the Engliſh.

Cambray, March 2. Count Morville, one of the French Plenipotentiaries, having received an Expreſs from his Court, ſet out this Day in his Return to Paris, but is quickly expected here again. We impatiently long to hear what Reſolution will be taken by the Court of Madrid, upon the Act of the Emperor, for the Inveſtiture of the States of Tuſcany, Parma and Placentia. Some are of Opinion, that this Project will prove agreeable to the Catholick King, and that the Cambray-Congreſs will not be terminated without a Peace between the Courts of Vienna and Madrid.

From the Harlem Courant.

Liſbon, Feb. 2. The Merchants at Bahir have tranſmitted a Petition to the King, praying the Fleet may not ſail from hence till next Year, by reaſon, that they are over-ſtock'd with European Goods.

Paris, March 6. The King ſeems to be fully inclined to follow the Maxims of the Court, according to what was practiſed by his Great Grandfather; for the Dutcheſs de Ventadour, late Governeſs of his Majeſty, and the Marſhal de Villeroy, took always great Pains to make the King believe, that the beſt Pattern he can follow in his Government is that of Lewis XIV.

Gibraltar, Feb. 5. The Traffick between this Town and Barbary is as good as re-eſtabliſhed. Two Ships arrived here lately from Tetuan, and having landed their Goods on Board without performing Quarantine, they returned Home. A French Ship from Tetuan is failed hence to Leghorn. Several of our Barks are ready to go to Barbary. Three Engliſh Men of War continue in this Bay, as alſo ſeveral Merchant Ships of that Nation.

Hague, March 6. To Morrow the States of Holland and Weſt-Frieſland will be aſſembled. An Expreſs from Sweden is embarked for London.

LONDON, *March* 5.

We hear, that the Cloſe of the laſt Week the Reverend Dr. Stanhope was introduced to the King by the Right Honourable the Lord Chamberlain, and had the Honour to preſent to his Majeſty his Sermon preach'd before the Honourable Houſe of Commons on the 30th of January laſt, and was very graciouſly received.

Thomas Wyndham, of Hawkchurch, in the County of Dorſet, Eſq; was lately married to Mrs. Helyar, of Yately, in the County of Southampton, an Heireſs of a very great Fortune.

Brudenel Rook, Eſq; Son of General Rook of Iſleworth, is lately married to Mrs. Anne Millington, of Bartlett-ſtreet, a Lady of a conſiderable Fortune.

The Right Honourable the Earls of Buchan and Haddington are arrived in Town from Scotland.

This Evening the Body of Sir Chriſtopher Wren, Knt. lately deceaſed, is to be carried from his Houſe in St. James's-ſtreet, Weſtminſter, with great Funeral State and Solemnity, to be depoſited in the great Vault under the Dome of St. Paul's Cathedral. The Trophies proper on ſuch Occaſions will not be carried before the Hearſe, becauſe not allow'd to be ſet up in the ſaid Cathedral, to prevent any Damage from driving Nails or Spikes into the Walls thereof.

Laſt Week at the Seſſions at Hicks's-Hall, Samuel Crawthorn, a young Fellow of about 16 or 17 Years old, was indicted for aſſaulting Suſanna Coleſit, an Infant aged 4 Years and a half, with an Intent to raviſh her, and for giving her the foul Diſeaſe: That the Child had the ſaid Diſtemper in a virulent Degree, appear'd by the Oath of a noted Surgeon belonging to Kingſland Hoſpital, who had her ſalivated, and that the ſaid Crawthorne gave it her, appeared by other Evidences; ſo that he was found Guilty of the Indictment, and ſentenced to be whip'd at the Carts Tail from Hog-Lane in Shoreditch, to Shoreditch Church, to pay a Fine of 3 s. 4 d. and to be put to hard Labour in Bridewell for one Month.

On Saturday laſt upon calling over the Priſoners in the Jail of Newgate, William Riddleſden, now Priſoner there for returning from Tranſportation, was brought to the Bar of the Court at the Old Bailey; but the ſaid Riddleſden having by a *Certiorari*, removed the Record of his former Conviction to the Court of King's-Bench, Weſtminſter, he is to be try'd there next Term.

Yeſterday they began to print the 75,000 Tickets of the New State Lottery at the Banquetting Houſe.

The great South-Sea Ship the Royal George, is arrived in the Downs from Falmouth.

On Sunday laſt one Winkles, ſummoning Bailiff

THE WHITEHALL EVENING POST, No. 700, March 2-5, 1723 (400 x 285mm).

were arrested by a general warrant for "seditious libel" because of an insinuation that the King had deliberately lied. The courts threw out all charges and the government tacitly accepted defeat in its battle to prevent the reporting of Parliament. Shackles were again put on newspaper publishers in the 1790s; and newspapers did not become free of overt Government interference until well into the nineteenth century.

George Crabbe the poet, celebrated in verse the number of newspapers available in the 1760s and 1770s:

> . . . soon as the morning dawns with roseate hue
>
> The "Herald" of the morn arises too,
> "Post" after "Post" succeeds, and all day long,
> "Gazettes" and "Ledgers" swarm, a motley throng . . .

The *Morning Chronicle* (1769-1862) was edited from 1774 to 1789 by William "Memory" Woodfall. Woodfall's nickname came from his astonishing ability of listening to a speech and then committing it, with great accuracy, to paper. When he parted with the *Chronicle*, he utilised this ability to produce the *Diary; or, Woodfall's Register* (1789-1793?), day-after reports of the proceedings in Parliament. His older brother, Henry Sampson Woodfall, edited the *Public Advertiser* (1752-1798) until 1793 gaining lasting fame for the paper for its inclusion of the anonymously written "Letters of Junius" from 1767-1772. The *Morning Post*, started in 1772 by John Bell, continued until 1937 when it amalgamated with the *Daily Telegraph*. *Johnson's British Gazette, and Sunday Monitor* (1779) was the first Sunday paper; The *Observer* (founded 1791) is the oldest to have survived. The *World* and the *Oracle* appeared in 1787 and 1789; the *Morning Herald*, started in 1780, survived until 1869 and the *Morning Advertiser* was established in 1794 by the Licensed Victuallers Association to maintain

Duty Stamp
Half penny
May 1716

THE
EDINBURGH Evening Courant.

From Monday Auguſt 29. to Tueſday Auguſt 30. 1726.

NUMB. XVIII.

The Country Gentleman.

Principiis Obſta.

Monday, May 9. 1726.

T is a hard Matter to reſiſt the Importunity of One's Friends, eſpecially when they are back'd by ſo prevailing an Advocate as Curioſity. This was my Caſe t'other Day, when *Will Teſty* and one of my Secretaries, who is a Maſter of Languages came to ſee me, and made me promiſe I wou'd go along with them to the Opera. When we came there, we found a prodigious Number of People drawn together to ſee two of the moſt famous Singers in *Europe, Cuzzoni* and *Fauſtina.* The latter comes to us with ſo ſuperior a Character That one might expect to hear from her, in Reality whatever the Poets of Old have feigned of *Amphion, Orpheus,* or the *Sirens. Will* adviſed me, to laſh my ſelf to one of the Poſt of the Gallery, where we ſate, as *Ulyſſes* did on the like Occaſion, to prevent any Accident, that might happen to me from the Power of her Incantations ; but I apprehended not any Danger from this New Comer, having found no ill Effects in the ſweet Captivity of *Cuzzoni.*

In a little Time, a Murmur ſpread it ſelf all over the Houſe, and every Body ſeemed to be engaged for one or other of theſe two great Rivals in *Harmony ;*

but as the Generality of the World is fond of Novelty, the Advocates for *Fauſtina* ſeemed to be much the greater Number. Some Ladies, who ſate near us, were very partial indeed, and ſaid, There was as much Difference between them as there was between Mrs *Robinſon* and *Boſchi* ; but Nobody equal'd an *Italian* in the Fulneſs of Praiſe, who (ſpeaking of *Fauſtina*) broke out into this Expreſſion ————— which my Secretary told us was in Engliſh

While we were thus entertained by the different Opinions of the People about us, we were joyn'd by my Poet, whoſe Curioſity had brought him to ſee this Dramatick Performance : He told us, That the Ingenious foreign Bard, the Compiler of this *Opera,* intended, at firſt, to adapt the Action to the European Manners, and therefore had married *Alexander* only to one of theſe Queens; but it ſeems the other Lady was reſolved (ſhe wou'd not be put off ſo ; it being beneath theDignity of her high Station to be ſlighted in ſuch a Manner ; and knowing her ſelf to be every Way qualified for a Wife, as well as the other : Upon this Remonſtance he was ordered to marry them both to this great Prince ; but he like a wiſe Man, underſtanding that *Bigamy,* in this Country, is Felony by the Law, refuſed to do it, not knowing, what Penalties an Acceſſary, in ſuch a Caſe, might be liable to. As this was thought a very Reaſonable Plea, he was in Hopes the Matter might be accommodated by marrying neither of them, and ſo leave them to ſhift for themſelves, as well as they cou'd in the Opinion of the World ; But it is a very nice Matter to decide in the Affairs of Princes ; And it ſeems our Bard had never in the leaſt, conſulted the Genius of the *Emperor :* For no ſooner had this Uxorious King Intelligence, that he was ſtill to continue a Batchelor, and to be deprived of thoſe ſweet Hopes, which he conceived to belong to a Conjugal State, but he gave a Looſe to his Paſſion, and wou'd have killed him, as ſure as he did his old Miniſter *Clytus,* but that his Javelin happened not to be pointed; it being a Maxim in *Dramatick Opera Chivalry,* not to ſuffer any of their Heroes

THE EDINBURGH EVENING COURANT, No. CXCV (195), August 29-30, 1726 (240 x 195mm)

their asylum. The first daily evening paper, the *Star and Evening Advertiser* of 1788 reverted to morning publication the following year but continued until 1831 until its merger with the *Albion*.

In 1785 there were eight morning papers in London. One of these, founded on New Year's Day, was the *Daily Universal Register* which, three years later, changed its name to *The Times*.

While the British press was firmly establishing itself during the eighteenth century, American journalism spent the same period catching up. The first paper to keep going in North America was the weekly *Boston News-Letter* 1704 published by the postmaster John Campbell, and distributed as a public service; in style and size it was very much like the *London Gazette*. In 1721 James, elder brother of Benjamin, Franklin started the *New-England Courant* in Boston to challenge the *News-Letter*.

Printed news spread slowly through the old colonies: Philadelphia's first newspaper appeared in 1719, the *American Weekly Mercury,* founded by Andrew Bradford. Benjamin Franklin, moving from Boston to Philadelphia in 1723 after a dispute with his brother, founded his *Pennsylvania Gazette* in 1728. New York's first paper was established by Andrew Bradford's father, William, in 1725, the *New-York Gazette*.

The right to criticise the government was accepted after John Peter Zenger's acquittal on a charge of libel in his *New-York Weekly Journal* 1735 and, by the War of Independence of 1775, almost forty newspapers were being published weekly or monthly, divided into patriot or royalist allegiance.

After Independence came the first dailies; the thrice-weekly *Pennsylvania Packet* turned daily in September 1784; its improved layout with clearly headed advertisements on the front page made it superior to, rather than imitative of, London papers. New York's *Daily Advertiser* followed the next year.

Duty Stamp
Half penny
August 1743

Opposite:
THE MORNING
POST
No. 920
October 7, 1775
(455 x 304mm)

THE PUBLIC
ADVERTISER
No. 13785
December 14, 1778
(458 x 290mm)

THE DAILY
UNIVERSAL
REGISTER
No. 1
January 1, 1785
(480 x 303mm)

Three typical newspapers of the
1770s and 80s: The Morning
Post *founded 1772 by John*
Bell; The Public Advertiser
1752-1798 and the inaugural
issue of the Daily Universal
Register *1785, which three*
years later changed its name to
The Times.

By the end of the century most of the larger cities had a daily newspaper, smaller towns a weekly. The drive to the west was still to come and the first paper west of the Mississippi was the *Missouri Gazette* published in St Louis in 1808.

Canada's newspapers also followed colonisation from east to west. The first printing presses arrived in the country in 1751 and, within a year, John Bushell published the first newspaper, the *Halifax Gazette* on 23 March 1752. Bushell's successor, Anthony Henry, continued to publish the *Gazette* until 1766 when he was deprived of the right to print because of his failure to pay Stamp Duty. Two years later, Henry established the rival *Nova Scotia Chronicle and Weekly Advertiser* which soon took enough custom from the *Gazette*, because of its lower price, to force the Gazette's owner to retire, leaving Henry open ground for his renamed *Nova Scotia Gazette and Weekly Chronicle.*

In June 1764 William Brown and Thomas Gilmore set up a press in Quebec and, with a subscribers list of 143, founded the *Quebec Gazette,* which continued publication until 1874. All the content was printed in both French and English.

La Gazette Litteraire 1778 was Montreal's first paper. It lasted barely a year before the proprietor, Fleury Mesplet, landed in gaol for his attacks on the government. The *Royal St John's Gazette* was the first to appear in New Brunswick in 1784, and in Ontario, the *Upper Canada Gazette, or American Oracle* was founded with the encouragement of the British Lieutenant-Governor in 1793.

It was almost another century before newspapers spread right across the continent, British Columbia having its first in the *Victoria Gazette* in 1858. The last state to have its own paper was Alberta where the *Edmonton Bulletin* was published in 1880 with 200 subscribers.

THE COUNTRY JOURNAL
No. 249
April 10, 1731
(354 x 272mm)

TIT-BITS
No. 53 Vol. III
October 21, 1882
(300 x 230mm)

1790-1890
MASS
CIRCULATION:
"KNOWLEDGE
IS POWER"

In the nineteenth century, the newspaper grew from a limited circulation news sheet for the educated elite into a technically developed, mass-circulation medium of entertainment; but before the circulations could rise, or the content of the newspapers expand, the battle between government and press had to be settled, and the technology of printing become more sophisticated.

William Pitt, Prime Minister from 1783 to 1801, sought to suppress free political expression at a time when popular agitation against the established order was growing. Editors and printers were charged with "seditious libel" as a regular occurrence: there were 200 such charges pending in 1792. In 1798, the *Courier's* proprietor John Parry was fined £100 and given six months in gaol for making a small mistake in reporting the restrictions on the export of timber to Russia. Printing presses were smashed, journalists transported. Foreign news, particularly sensitive matters such as the progress of the French Revolution, was blocked by forcing it to pass through official censors. Compliant newspapers would get information from government sources, recalcitrant ones would not. The government paid money to proprietors in order to buy their support. In Ireland it employed agents to take over dissident journals. *The Times* in its early years received £300 per annum and, in common with other papers, accepted political bribes to remove offensive reports. Advertisement and Stamp Taxes were increased in the 1790s with higher penalties for evasion.

Inevitably, after such an onslaught of direct and indirect pressure, circulations were forced down — the *Morning Post,* for instance, was only selling 350 copies per day in 1795. A circulation of 2,000 was regarded as high. Hatred of the restrictions by a handful of newspaper owners and journalists, and their active opposition to the government, enabled an independent press to

The Dublin Chronicle

Price. Two-Pence.   TUESDAY, NOVEMBER 1, 1791.

IRISH STATE LOTTERY, 1791,
Commences Drawing on the 14th NOVEMBER next.

ARTHUR GRUEBER,

RESPECTFULLY informs his Friends and the Public, that he is now felling TICKETS and SHARES in the greatest variety of Numbers and at the lowest rates,

AT THE GOVERNMENT LOTTERY OFFICE
No. 59. Dame-street.

The TICKETS are divided into
HALVES   EIGHTHS,
QUARTERS,   SIXTEENTHS,
and GUINEA TICKETS,
by which a good may be gained.
All duly Stamped agreeable to Act of Parliament.

The full Money allowed for Prizes in the late English and Irish Lotteries, in exchange for Tickets, or Country orders, remitting good bills, executed on the fame Terms as for Money at the Government Lottery Office, No. 59, Dame-street, by   ARTHUR GRUEBER.

NEW BOOKS published this Day, by J. JONES, No. 111, Grafton-street, opposite the College.

1. Buffon's Natural History, abridged, including the History of the Elements—the Earth and its component parts—Mountains, Rivers, Seas, Winds, Whirlwinds, Waterspouts, Volcanoes, Earthquakes—History of Man, Quadrupeds, Birds, Fishes, Shell-fishes, Lizards, and Serpents, with a general View of the Insect World, illustrated with upwards of 100 Figures neatly engraved on copper-plates. Price neatly bound, only 8s. 8d. boards 7s. 6d.

2. Celestina, a new Novel, by C. Smith, 3 Vols.   9 9
3. Wenslingham's View of England towards the close of the 18th Century, 2 Vols.   -   6 6
4. Danith Massacre, an Historic Fact   -   J J
5. Bennett's Strictures on Female Education   2 8½
6. The History of Miss Meredith, by Mrs. Parfon   J J
7. The Next Door Neighbours, a Comedy, by Mrs. Inchbald   -   -   -   -   6h

HEALTH AND LONGEVITY.

Dr. JAMES's ANALEPTIC PILLS.

TO preserve Health, and of course to prolong Life, nothing is so necessary as an attention to those flight indispositions to which all men are subject, and which, by being considered as trifling, are too often disregarded, till by neglect they lay deep root in the constitution, and become of serious and sometimes fatal consequence. These complaints whether the cause of them be a cold, excess of eating or drinking, fatigue of body or mind, a too active or too sedentary life, a guilty or bilious disposition, &c. &c. are generally discovered by some obstructions in the minute vessels, or by some defect in the natural secretions.—As a remedy for these evils, the celebrated inventor of the Fever Powder compounded this Analeptic Pills, and he exhibited in himself a memorable instance of their efficacy; for by the constant use of them, though a free liver, he attained to the age of seventy-five.

The tendency of the Septis is to up in the pores by night and the body by day. They remove obstructions, promote sleep, and they require neither confinement nor attention to diet. They are also an admirable remedy for rheumatic disorders, for the head ach, and for those complaints to which the female sex are peculiarly subject.

They should be taken on the first attack of a cold, and upon all occasions of uneasiness or indisposition, and should never be omitted at bed-time after any excess.

They are sold only by J. JONES, No. 111, Grafton-street, Dublin, in boxes at 4s. 9d. each, where may be had Dr. James's Fever Powder, in packets at 2s. 6d. each—Likewise Dr. Snape's Infallible Powder for most disorders in horses, in packets at 2s. 9d. each; and Irwin's Fruit Lozenges, prepared without sugar, so well known for their great efficacy in curing of colds, coughs, and hoarsenesses, &c. &c.

N. B. Every new book, play and pamphlet to be had as soon as published at J. JONES's.

TO THE PUBLIC.

THE LIONS OFFICE, No. 101, Grafton-street, being Licensed for the Sale of Tickets and Shares in the present Irish Lottery,—The Public are respectfully informed that all business as warranted by Act of Parliament will be transacted with Correctness and Honor.

The Number and Amount of the Prizes paid in former Lotteries by

Mr. LE FAVRE,

are too well known to trouble the Public with more.

The same care and fairness of dealing that first gained Public patronage to the LIONS OFFICE, will be firmly observed to all who Honour it with their Commands. No. 101, Grafton-street,

14th October, 1791.

The full value paid at the Counter for Mr. Le Favre's outstanding Prizes.

This Day is published, (Price 4s. 10½d.)
At SLEATER's, Dame-street,

TABLES of LATITUDE and DEPARTURE, with an Essay on their Origin and Use; particularly as they are suited to the Purposes of Land Surveying; Also, an Appendix, containing an illustration of all the Methods of Calculation hitherto practised, and a Specimen of Eight New Methods, never before published,

By THOMAS HARDING.

Designed to reduce Calculation from the intricacy and Obscurity in which it was too long involved; an impartial Examination of the Notes and Remarks on the various Methods hitherto published, will shew how far the Author's Endeavours have been successful.

The practical Surveyor, who would wish to be decided by Arithmetical Calculation, WHICH CANNOT ERR, will find this small Volume his best Companion, and his Employers can, of course, experience at their best Friends.

NEW BOOKS.
This Day is published
By W. SLEATER, No. 26, Dame-street,

CELESTINA,
A NOVEL

By Charlotte Smith,
In 3 Volumes.

Price sewed 8s. 2d.h.—Neatly bound 9s. 9d.

SACRED EXTRACTS, or books and chapters selected from the Old and New Testaments, for the use of schools. Price neatly bound 4s. 4d.

A Compendium of Ancient and Modern Historical Geography by Mr. de Lanleau, Price 2s. 9d. bound.

Next Door Neighbours, a Comedy. 6d.h.

The Kentish Barons, a Comedy. 6d.h.

Every New Publication at W. SLEATER's.

STRIKING LIKENESSES IN MINIATURE PROFILE.

By J. THOMASON, at No. 31, Great South George's-street, Dublin, in Gilt Frames, at 6s. 6d. each.

HE thanks the Public for their kind patronage, humbly hopes the improvement he has made since his arrival, in the size, finish, and animation of his Profiles, will secure him a continuance thereof. In order to accommodate persons who have business in the Country who do not come to Town, he will give printed instructions for taking their Shades themselves, which may be sent to him to be reduced, dressed and set without any additional charge.—His instructions are given with so much simplicity and ease that a child cannot mistake them. No Likenesses but what are approved need be sent, which he will engage to preserve.

N. B. Old Shades copied or reduced.—Rooms open from ten till seven in the evening.

Time of Sitting one minute only.

This Day is published,
At SLEATER's, Dame-street.
(Price 3d. or 1l. 2s. 9d. per Hundred)

BRITAIN's HAPPINESS and its full Possession of Civil and Religious Liberty, briefly stated and proved.

By the late Rev. Dr. RICHARD PRICE.
With an Introduction by the Editor.

ROBERT BURNETT,
PAINTER, PAPER-STAINER, and STUCCO-WORKER,
No. 190, Great Britain-street, Dublin.
(Who served his Time to the late Mr. John Baptist Coville)

RESPECTFULLY informs the Nobility and Gentry, that he executes the above branches of Business in the newest fashion and most approved manner; and having been employed by some of the first Families in this Kingdom, he can satisfy any Gentleman of the superior excellence of his Work; which, with moderate charges, will, he hopes, be his strongest recommendation.

As BURNETT has been at considerable expence in selecting a large and fashionable variety of Paper Hangings, which he can engage, he recompences them to the notice of the Public.—Great encouragement to those who buy to sell again, and for exportation.
Plain Rooms neatly coloured.

N. B. BURNETT will execute any branch of his Business in the Country at Dublin Prices.

To the FRIENDS of LITERATURE and the ARTS in IRELAND.

Proposals for Printing by Subscription,
By RANDAL M'ALLISTER, BOOKSELLER,
NO. 102, GRAFTON-STREET,

NATURAL HISTORY, GENERAL and PARTICULAR, by the COUNT de BUFFON, translated into English, illustrated with above 300 Copper-plates, and containing Notes and Observations, by William Smellie, Member of the Antiquarian and Royal Societies of Edinburgh.

CONDITIONS

1. This Work shall be elegantly printed on a fine Paper, with above 300 Copper-plates, engraved by the best Artists; to be comprised in 9 Vols. large 8vo.

2. The Price to Subscribers, three Guineas; one Guinea to be paid at the Time of subscribing, the Remainder on Delivery of the Work, in Boards; which will be put to Press with all convenient speed. The Price to Non-Subscribers three Guineas and a-half.

3. The Subscribers Names shall be printed, as Encouragers of Literature and the Arts in Ireland.

Subscriptions will be received by the Publisher, RANDAL M'ALLISTER, No. 102, Grafton-street, and by the principal Booksellers in Ireland.

⁎ The Work now offered to the Public is a Translation of the celebrated Productions of the COUNT de BUFFON, and the Result of the Labour of more than twenty Years, which for a considerable Length of time has stood the Test of the candid Examination, and earned universal Admiration of the Learning, Taste, Genius, and Eloquence which it displays. All the Stores of Nature have been largely investigated towards its Completion, and the Judgment and Ability uniformly exhibited by the sagacious Author, have insured the approach of the learned and judicious throughout Europe. Convinced hitherto, partly by the Language in which it was conceived, but more by its Price (amounting at the lowest to Twenty Guineas) to the Cabinets of the wealthy and the great, it is now proposed to present the curious investigators of Nature with a Translation of it in their native Tongue at a very moderate Rate. As no Science is more instructive, so none is more entertaining than Natural History; it is, in Fact, the principal Source from which Human Knowledge is derived. The Abilities of the Translator are confessedly superior; and he has introduced various Notes and Illustrations that add much to the information and considerable Value to the MAGNIFICENT WORK of the ILLUSTRIOUS BUFFON. As the Editor pledges himself that the Plates, Paper, and Press-Work shall do credit to his Country, he confidently relies on the Support of the Friends of the Arts in Ireland, whose Patronage he will endeavour to merit by his best Exertions.—The Spirit of this Undertaking is at least Praise-worthy; the Execution of the Public can alone render it effectual.

keep alive. William Cobbett, 'writer and publisher for the people', was one of the men to bear the flag of independence. After living in America from 1792 to 1800, he returned to England apparently a staunch Tory, but by 1804 he had shifted his political ground dramatically to the popular reforming side. Undoubtedly his hatred of government control of the press was an important factor in Cobbett's change of direction. His short-lived *Porcupine* (1800-1801) was rabidly anti-French, anti-republican, but his *Weekly Political Register* (1802-1835) soon changed its stance. The *Register* was a remarkable paper, edited and largely written by Cobbett in an almost unbroken run until his death. It was a small format, book-size paper of sixteen pages summarising political events and subjecting them to radical comment. Cobbett wrote that:

> The Press which has been called the Palladium of the free man has, like many other things in our political state, been so completely perverted as to become one of the chief means by which freedom . . . has been nearly extinguished amongst us.

His criticism of the flogging of 500 militiamen for complaining about their rations earned Cobbett a fine and a two-year prison sentence in 1810, but he still continued to edit the *Register* while in gaol. Leigh Hunt, in his *Examiner,* 1813, criticised the Prince Regent and spent a similar period behind bars as a result.

Underhand methods were used by the government to silence questioning voices. *Agents provocateurs* trapped newspapers by providing them with false reports, which they were then prosecuted for publishing. The Stamp Tax was increased to 4d in 1815, but again there was a St. George to slay the dragon. William Hone, a publisher of scurrilous pamphlets, brought out his *Reformist's Register* in 1817 and soon crossed

Opposite:
THE DUBLIN
CHRONICLE
No. 706
November 1, 1791
(300 x 236mm)

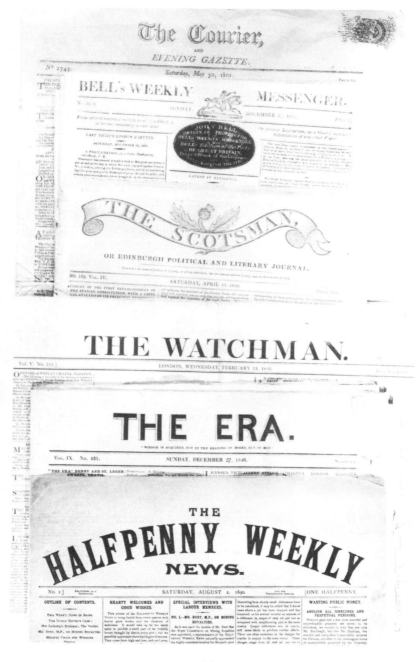

swords with the law. His parodies of well-known sections of the Prayer Book were proceeded against for their profanity rather than their sedition, but after the famous "The Three Trials of William Hone", in which he ran rings round the prosecution, he was acquitted. This strange charade, which entertained everyone except the government, took place only a short time after Thomas Barnes became editor of *The Times* in 1817.

Thomas Barnes was the one man who, more than any other, transformed British journalism in the nineteenth century. His first task was to continue the process of extricating his paper from a position of subservience to political party and the state. His aim was to make *The Times* an opinion-forming leader of people and governments.

Technically, the paper was advanced. In 1814 it had been the first in the world to use the new reel-fed Koenig Press, producing 1,000 copies an hour, rather than the wood and iron, hand operated flat-bed machines which limited production to 20 an hour, although each copy still had to be folded by hand, like all broadsheet newspapers until late in the century.

When Barnes took over *The Times*, its circulation was 7,000; soon it reached 15,000. He explained his successful philosophy in the 1830s:

> John Bull, whose understanding is rather sluggish — I speak of the majority of readers — requires a strong stimulus. He consumes his beef and cannot digest it without a dram. He dozes composedly over his prejudices which his conceit calls opinions, and you must fire ten-pounders at his densely compacted intellect before you can make it comprehend your meaning or care a farthing for your efforts.

This was satirised, at least partially, because of its successful application. An 1830 cartoon

Opposite:
THE COURIER
No. 2745
May 30, 1801
(492 x 332mm)

BELL'S WEEKLY
MESSENGER
No. 1029
December 17, 1815
(390 x 265mm)

THE SCOTSMAN
No. 169
April 15, 1820
(363 x 264mm)

THE WATCHMAN
No. 215
February 13, 1839
(520 x 390mm)

THE ERA
No. 431
December 27, 1846
(456 x 304mm)

THE HALF-PENNY
WEEKLY NEWS
No. 1
August 2, 1890
(450 x 304mm)

showed "John Bull or the Man Wot is Easily Led by the Nose", and there he is, his nose linked by a chain with a copy of *The Times* spread out before him and exclaiming: "What a glorious thing is to enjoy the liberty and independence of an Englishman".

The Times' success was aided by increasing advertising revenue. At the same time, in the years before the 1832 Reform Act, British politics was in a state of upheaval. Barnes was not willing to be bought, and supported or rejected legislation brought before Parliament as he thought fit. When Barnes died in 1841, the "Thunderer", as *The Times* was popularly called, was selling 28,000 copies. This was almost as many as the rest of the opposition papers put together, and four times the circulation of the "Grunticle", Barnes' name for the *Morning Chronicle* which, only a few years before, had been *The Times'* greatest rival. The removal of restrictions on the size of paper in 1825 and the reductions in Advertisement and Stamp Taxes in 1833 and 1836, culminating in their removal in 1855, must largely be credited to Barnes and his insistent, and successful, newspaper publishing policies, although *The Times* itself was eventually to suffer because of the increased competition that resulted.

While the "Thunderer" attracted readers at the higher end of the market, the nineteenth century also brought in with it the popular press. The first new newspaper of the century was the *Weekly Dispatch* (1801) which declared itself to be "at once instructive and entertaining". In that dictum it can be linked directly with the "ha'penny press" of the 1890s. In terms of price it was still expensive at 8d, though its rivals sold at 9d or 10d including tax. The *Dispatch* covered sports and trials, which entertained a wider market. Its rivals carried mere snippets of news hidden away amongst the advertisements and leading articles.

A typical issue of the *Morning Post*, for 3 July 1804, for instance, contained advertisements, a report on Parliament and shipping news in its four pages. In the small amount of space remaining were to be found only a couple of news items: comments on the possibility of Bonaparte invading England, and a note on two kangaroos at Pidcock's Royal Menagerie. Together with a few births, marriages and corn prices, that was it.

In the 1820s and 1830s other popular weeklies were launched. The *Sunday Times* of 1822 (which, confusingly, grew out of the *New Observer*, founded 1821 with an intermediate title of the *Independent Observer*) soon achieved a reputation for its sensational and salacious reporting. The *Observer* (founded 1791) was originally a staid, heavy Sunday paper, but in the 1820s also turned its attention to crime and sport. The *News of the World* entered the sensation stakes in 1843 and, priced at 3d, aimed itself exclusively and unequivocally at the great mass of people. By January 1845 its circulation was 17,500 every Sunday, and by the end of that year it was 30,000. Its eight pages contained no illustrations but had news conveniently grouped under headings: Foreign news under countries, Country news under towns; Literature, Varieties, Police, Letters to the Editor, Advice to Readers ("J.V. Newcastle — We have not the slightest idea as we never use cosmetics ourselves"), and so on. The price was still 3d:

> There is only ¼d profit upon each copy of the paper to cover all the expenses of editorship, printing, &c. Unexampled in merit and unparalleled in price, its price shall never be more than 3d. THAT IS OUR FIXED AND IRREVOCABLE INTENTION.

The newspaper from which the *News of the World* gained its inspiration was an earlier

Newspaper Duty Stamp 1836

THE

POOR MAN'S GUARDIAN,
A Weekly Paper
FOR THE PEOPLE.

PUBLISHED IN DEFIANCE OF " LAW," TO TRY THE POWER
OF " RIGHT " AGAINST " MIGHT."

" IT IS THE CAUSE; IT IS THE CAUSE."

No. 42.]　　　　Saturday, March 31, 1832.　　　　[Price 1d.

Friends, Brethren, and Fellow-Countrymen,

On Thursday night HOBHOUSE, the " baronet who has got a place," gently expostulated with CROKER for calling the people of England " insatiable wild beasts "—would to God they were instead of the tame beasts they are, satisfied with anything—any cruelty—any indignity their masters may please to put upon them! were they so, they would at any rate be more feared and better treated, if not more respected. This was a charge, however, which would, some years ago, have roused the radical member for Westminster beside himself:—but place and time have done much to cool his liberality, and he now merely *expostulated*, when formerly he would have ranted for an hour—But all this goes for nothing—CROKER " explained " to the apparent satisfaction of the radical Hobhouse, and of the other house too—this Whig reforming house—who love the poor labouring classes and intend so much good—And how did he explain?—take the words of the " legitimate newspapers " for it.

" Mr. CROKER said, the Right Hon. Baronet said he had called the People of England insatiable wild beasts. It was the *Populace*, not of the *People*, of whom he was speaking at the time."

And to this there was no reply from any of your liberal reformers! You—you are " the *populace*—the mob as contradistinguished from the PEOPLE," as that arch hypocrite—the times-serving Brougham told you—you are " *cut off from among the people !* " you must look for no privileges of men, you are objects to be insulted with impunity by any coward who has risen into power by truckling up the steps of dishonesty and injustice! this CROKER too who has fatted, in abject and slavish sloth, upon the very best of what you have been tame enough to create for the exclusive advantage of those, the like of him—by labour harder than that of *beasts*—and which too you are " *insatiable* " enough to see others enjoy to profusion while you starve who have produced!—" *Wild !*" " *Insatiable !!* " " *Beasts !!!* " You ought to be *wild* :—let CROKER turn *weaver* for a day and a year and keep himself and family on seven shillings a week ;—would not he be wild ?—would not he find himself worse than a " beast ? "—and would he, withall, be satisfied ?—is he satisfied *now* on his thousands? would not even he get more if he could ?—we should be sorry to be a good sinecure in his way! And what right has any man to call his fellow insatiable who puts up with less than himself! Vengeance is a sweet compensation, and the day will be ours yet when we may teach these Whigs what " insatiable wild beasts " we are.—We warrant we shall —though we are the *many* and they the *few*—be satisfied altogether with less of their blood than daily sufficeth them of ours—which they spill like water and live and fatten on! We warrant that our *wildness* shall have more moderation and justice in it than their *civilization* !—and, *beasts* as we are, we will treat our conquered tyrants more like *men*, than they treat *us* who, so far from wronging them, slave in misery and privation for their sole benefit and pleasure! when will that day arrive !—But until that day arrives let this insult put upon you, and allowed by your liberal, fine-promising, and fair-speaking reformers, put you upon your guard as to their intentions : do they ever intend you to be emancipated? do they ever intend *reform* for the mob and " insatiable wild beasts?" BROUGHAM has long told you that you who are rational beings, are not of the people—you, who were not so despicable but *he* always found your applause a serviceable *honour*, and worth the address of his most " liberal " eloquence—you, whose shouts were not so base but they have raised him to his present eminence! BROUGHAM had long told you *his* views of you,—but it remained for the Whig house to adopt them :—and now they have;—they too think you unworthy to be ranked among the PEOPLE,—they look on you as " mob " and populace,—as, in fact, " insatiable wild beasts ! " and is it probable that thinking thus of you, they will ever admit you to equal privileges with themselves—ever make their superiorities and advantages dependant upon your " sweet voices ? "—think it not ; they have no intention of extending the benefits of *reform* to you : open your eyes, we beg of you, for your own sake; be prepared for deceit—do not assist *duplicity* to make fools of you; nor, at any rate, be disappointed when you find that you have gained nothing.

Sunday: *Bell's Life in London and Sporting Chronicle*, founded in 1822. Billed as containing:

> News of the Week. A Rich Repository of Fashion, Wit and Humour and the Interesting Incidents of Real Life.

It was published "at 4 o'clock on Saturday afternoon so that it might be had on Sunday within 200 miles of London" and was priced at 7d. Its centre pages contained columns on various subjects each headed by a woodcut. Answers to Correspondents, The Fashionable World, The Drama, Pet's Corner, Sporting Chronicle, The Turf and Police Intelligence.

All these "legitimate" newspapers included Stamp Tax in the cover price and carried the government's red stamp to show it. However, until the reduction of the tax to 1d in 1836, many unstamped newspapers flourished outside the law. Some refused to pay the tax on principle, like Henry Hetherington, publisher of the *Poor Man's Guardian* which was founded in 1831, price 1d. Hetherington went to prison on several occasions because he would not pay. He established his paper "contrary to 'Law' to try the Power of 'Might' against 'Right' ". Instead of the official duty stamp was an imitation proclaiming "Knowledge is Power" and showing a printing press. The *Guardian* aimed to protect and uphold the

Left:
THE POOR MAN'S
GUARDIAN
No. 42
March 31, 1832
(248 x 184mm)
Many of the unstamped newspapers and periodicals of the 1830s avoided stamp tax as long as possible then went out of business. Henry Hetherington, proprietor of the Guardian *made it a campaigning issue. His refusal to pay meant several periods in prison.*

> key to all our liberties — the Freedom of the Press — the press too of the IGNORANT and the POOR! We will never abandon our post; we will die rather. The fight is begun!

Other unstamped papers just imitated *Bell's Life in London* and hoped to undercut the stamped press by selling at only a penny. They proliferated to such an extent that the Stamp Office had a special team of detectives to track them down. The *Penny Satirist* of 1837 described itself as "a cheap substitute for a weekly paper". It was full of "remarkable stories" like the one about a seaman who seemed to be a woman, was made companion to the captain's wife, and was then exposed as a man after all, the captain's wife's lover. The *Penny Sunday Times* and *People's Gazette* had large front-page cartoons and a generally more interesting and progressive layout than the stamped press.

A simple list of just a few of these underground papers makes exciting reading in itself; *Slap at the Church, Destructive, Working Man's Friend, Voice of the People, Political Soldier, Scourge, Weekly Show-Up, Libel, Liar, Squib, Wag, Thief, Scab, Quizzing Glass, Patriot, Man in the Moon, Fool's-Cap, Cosmopolite.*

In 1835 there were 219 prosecutions against the sellers of unstamped journals, but the last came in February 1836 when, incidentally, unstamped sales outstripped those of the stamped.

But with duty reduced to 1d most of the Great Unstamped went out of business, their price now being only slightly lower and no longer sufficient to make up for lower quality. *The News of the World*'s excellence and cheapness contributed to this, while the Chartist newspaper, the *Northern Star* ("The Charter and No Surrender!") and the Socialist *New Moral World* attracted much of the radical readership.

Two imitation 'tax' stamps from the Poor Man's Guardian *and* Cleave's Penny Gazette, *July 30, 1842.*

72

Above all this *The Times*, which, under the editorship of John Delane between 1841 and 1877 reached sales of 70,000, argued against the total removal of the Stamp Tax. Although this might seem odd at first glance, *The Times* was by now a bulky paper and the tax allowed papers to be sent through the post free of charge. *The Times* had most to lose and probably lost more than it ever expected. After the abolition of the tax in 1855, the *Manchester Guardian* (founded 1821) and other provincial papers went daily for the first time. The *Daily Telegraph*, founded two weeks after the abolition on 29 June 1855 as the *Daily Telegraph and Courier,* reduced its price to a penny for eight pages in 1857. Its circulation was soon outstripping *The Times*, reaching 250,000 copies in the 1870s, at that time the biggest in the world for any periodical.

It took a long time before the visual effects of the Stamp Tax were shaken off. Headlines had been stifled when extra pages meant extra duty, but papers were also influenced by *The Times'* attitude that headlines and design were not important because, it was haughtily assumed, everyone would read from beginning to end anyway. Only in the 1880s and 1890s came the break away from the space-saving habits which had encouraged "acres of unrelieved print".

The mass-market for news was greatly enlarged by the Elementary Education Act of 1870. George Newnes was one of the first to realise the potential of this new generation of readers and translated his hobby for collecting cuttings from newspapers into a weekly periodical — *Tit-Bits* — founded in 1881: '3,500 tit-bits of news, information, jokes a year from numerous sources'. Within two hours 5,000 copies of the first issue were sold; three months after its launch it was selling 900,000 copies a week.

An important breakthrough in evening newspapers was made by W. T. Stead's *Pall Mall Gazette* 1865, followed by the *Echo* three years later. The *Daily Telegraph* had given impetus to betting on horse racing by publishing the racing results, and evening papers with a strong sporting side were in demand: the *St James's Gazette* began in 1880, the *Westminster Gazette* (published by Newnes as a Liberal Party paper) in 1893. News agencies such as Reuters, established 1847, and the Press Association, 1870, helped popular papers supply foreign news at a much lower cost than if each had to despatch its own reporters around the world. Cheaper newsprint and more efficient printing methods aided expansion.

The potential was there. *Tit-Bits* showed the popularity of the short, simple paragraph combined with gimmicks such as prize competitions and free accident insurance; the "New Journalism" of the *Pall Mall Gazette* and *The Star* of 1888, provided the topical news element. The "ha'penny press" of the 1890s saw the demand from the public, and supplied that public with the product it wanted. The newspaper industry was underway; and, for the first time, American newspapers influenced their British counterparts in both layout and content.

Writing in his magazine, the *Leisure Hour,* in April 1871, the editor reported on his "First impressions of American newspapers". 1,450 newspapers were published in the United Kingdom at the beginning of that year, 120 of them dailies. In America "with a population not much greater than our own" there were at least 5,200 newspapers, 550 of them dailies:

> Every town and nearly every village has its newspaper. So that, as to quantity, America is before all the world the land of newspapers . . . But what of the quality? I have no hestitation in affirming that, on the whole, it is as high as our own. They have no daily paper like our *Times*, but they have a hundred as good as any of our best papers excepting *The Times*.

The writer singles out, however, the *New York Herald* as of particularly "low moral tone", and in general criticises

> another obvious fault . . . the strain of exaggeration and the constant striving at "sensational" effects . . . Every paper aims at having starting and sensational announcements. Large capital headings sprawl down half a column.

Comparing the histories of the American and British press in the nineteenth century shows that there was a complete about-face; it started with Americans copying the style and printing methods of the British, but ended with the British lagging behind, copying American sensationalism and design.

New York's first penny paper, the *Sun* of 1833, was of staid enough appearance although it did not, like most other American papers, have its front page plastered with small advertisements. The *New York Herald* (founded by James Gordon Bennett in 1835) and the *New York Tribune*, 1841, both followed the heavy, largely headline-less, small-print, news pages.

The Civil War proved to be the spur for innovation and it was in the 1860s that the "multi-decker" headline developed with as many as ten or twelve mini-headings "sprawling down half a column".

In content the *Sun*, the *Herald* and the *Tribune* varied: the *Sun* was after a popular audience with "human interest" stories, the *Herald* provided entertainment first and foremost, and the *Tribune* took the rôle of the idealistic crusader. Other papers took on these, or similar, approaches; such rôle-playing — directing the content of the paper towards a particular readership and a particular goal — was largely unexplored at this stage by the British press. The *Chicago Times*, 1854, offered sensation in opposition to the *Chicago Tribune* of 1847, which emphasised civic pride; the *Kansas City Star*, 1880, investigated

75

and exposed corruption. Joseph Pulitzer's *St Louis Post-Despatch* of 1878 was perhaps the foremost crusading newspaper; in 1883 Pulitzer bought the failing *New York World* and in three years increased the circulation from 15,000 to 250,000 by combining sensationalism with crusading idealism.

By the end of the century, the newspaper wars, particularly in New York between Pulitzer's *World* and Randolph Hearst's *New York Journal* (purchased in 1895), helped create headlines and design which left Britain decades behind. Two years after the *Daily Mail* was launched in Britain, with its front pages filled with advertisements, the *Boston Daily Globe* was carrying headlines filling half the page. Visually exciting, the content *was* of a "low moral tone". Scare stories, pure lies and fabrications, comic strips and pictures formed what came to be known as "yellow journalism". In 1896, when Adolph S.

THE PENNY SATIRIST
No. 356
February 10, 1844
(490 x 370mm)
Satirical, radical and piratical;
essential ingredients of the
unstamped press.

Ochs took over the *New York Times,* he made capital out of his "yellow" rivals by making his paper a serious journal containing "all the news that's fit to print".

Australian and New Zealand newspaper history started only in the nineteenth century; the *Sydney Gazette* was the first paper, appearing on Saturday March 5th, 1803; a mixture of manuscript and type:

> Innumerable as the obstacles were which threatened to oppose our undertaking, yet we are happy to affirm that they were not insurmountable. The utility of PAPER in the COLONY, as it must open a source of solid information, will, we hope, be universally seen and acknowledged. We have courted the assistance of the Ingenious and the Intelligent . . . We open no channel to political discussion or personal animadversion. Information is our only purpose; that acknowledged we shall consider that we have done our duty in an exertion to merit the Approbation of the Public and to ensure a liberal patronage to the *Sydney Gazette.*

With the tone of a Royal Proclamation, Australia's first attempt at a newspaper announced itself to the world. It was an official publication, set up by Governor Philip King, and remained strictly so until George Howe, the printer, was granted freedom from censorship.

A number of short-lived newspapers appeared such as the *Derwent Star,* Hobart 1810, *Van Diemen's Land Gazette* 1814, but the *Hobart Town Gazette,* started as a manuscript newsletter in 1816, survived to become the *Tasmanian Government Gazette.* In Sydney a second paper was published in 1824-28, the *Australian,* which came out monthly with four pages like the Gazette, and a third, *The Monitor.* The *Sydney Morning Herald* of 1831 proved to be the most popular, increasing its circulation to more than its three rivals could muster between them. The *Herald* went daily in 1840.

In the 1830s, the manuscript newsletter, harking back to an earlier age in Europe, was still in existence. Copies were nailed to trees for public consumption. One of the first of these was the *Western Australia Gazette,* produced in Fremantle in 1830, each sheet selling for three shillings. Another, the *Fremantle Journal,* came out in 1832, the same year as the first printing press arrived in Western Australia which was used to produce the *West Australian News.* A particularly successful paper was the *Perth Gazette* of 1837, which later became the *West Australian.*

Victoria's first newspaper was the handwritten *Melbourne Advertiser,* 1838, thirty copies of each issue being published. It appeared in printed form the following year. At the same time two Port Phillip papers, the *Gazette* and the *Herald,* were launched. Queensland's *Moreton Bay Courier* of June 1846 was a forerunner of the Brisbane *Courier-Mail*

Three other notable Australian newspapers were the *Melbourne Argus,* under the editorship of Edward Wilson from 1848, the *Melbourne Herald,* 1849, and David Symes' *The Age,* 1854.

The first issue of the earliest New Zealand newspaper was printed in London in 1839 before emigrants left for the new colony. The second issue of 18 April 1840 was printed on New Zealand soil at Port Nicholson (now Wellington). The *New Zealand Advertiser* was published two months later in the Bay of Islands. The *Auckland Times,* first published in August 1842, was initially printed on a government press, but after nine issues this use was refused to the proprietor, Henry Falwasser, when his views failed to meet government approval. Falwasser continued to publish the aid of a mangle. The oldest surviving paper still published in New Zealand is the *Taranaki Herald* of 1852.

1890-1982 MODERN NEWSPAPERS: STRUGGLE FOR SURVIVAL

It the foundation of the *Daily Courant* and *The Times* were milestones in the earlier history of newspapers, the breakthrough to the truly modern press arrived with the *Daily Mail*, the "Penny Newspaper for One Halfpenny" in 1896. It was not the first "ha'penny" — it was preceded by the *Summary* 1883 and the *Morning* and *Morning Leader* of 1892 — but it was the most successful by far.

Alfred Harmsworth, founder of the *Mail*, became the first "newspaper baron", Lord Northcliffe. He revolutionised what went into the paper and at the same time started the process of buying and selling newspaper companies which has led to the grouping of almost all local and national daily and weekly papers into business conglomerates.

Northcliffe started by writing for Newnes' *Tit-Bits*. including a tit-bit on "How fortunes are made', for a guinea a column. By that time Newnes had already made his fortune, and Northcliffe set up his own weekly called *Answers*, in 1888, which extended Newnes original concept: "Interesting. Extraordinary. Amusing. Answers to Correspondents on Every Subject Under the Sun.' *Answers* was followed by other penny weeklies and Northcliffe, with his brother Harold Harmsworth (later Lord Rothermere) shared a million-pound publishing firm by 1895.

A year earlier, Northcliffe had purchased the *Evening News*, first published in 1881 and distinguished by the different coloured paper used for each edition, turning it into a worthy competitor of the *Star* which had led the six London evenings since its foundation in 1888.

The first issue of the *Daily Mail* of 4 May 1896 was described by its detractors as "printed by office boys for officeboys". To safeguard the secrecy of his project and, no doubt, to generate some healthy pre-launch publicity, Northcliffe ordered dummy copies of the paper to be

Night Special symbol from the EVENING NEWS, 1963

produced at intervals between February and May 1896. These dummies were "leaked" to outsiders, but their content and design were completely different from the final product. The scheme, and the quality of the real *Daily Mail,* secured a circulation of almost a million by 1900. At the same time *The Times* sold 38,000 at 3d and the *Manchester Guardian* 44,000 at 1d. The *Mail's* formula was spot-on: news and gossip in easily read paragraphs, women readers catered for for the first time, photographs used instead of line drawings and bigger headlines employed, though with advertisements on the front page.

Success soon had its emulators and C. Arthur Pearson, who had won a *Tit-Bits* competition prize of a place on the staff of the magazine, also went off, like Northcliffe, to set up a rival publication. *Pearson's Weekly,* 1890, was followed ten year's later by Pearson's *Daily Express* — with news on the front page. From then to now, the *Express* and *Mail* have been locked in a battle for readers.

In 1903, Northcliffe founded the *Daily Mirror* as a specifically female paper — "By Women, For Women". But despite a sale of 265,000 copies of the first issue, within three months its circulation was down to 25,000, the most dramatic drop in newspaper history. Northcliffe described it as

> the only journalistic failure with which I have been associated . . . Some people say that a woman never really knows what she wants. It is certain she knew what she didn't want. She didn't want the *Daily Mirror.*

He decided "to make an experiment with it". The price was changed to a halfpenny and the paper "filled full of photographs and pictures to see how that would do. It did.' Within a month circulation was up to 143,000 per day. The *Daily Illustrated Mirror* (soon contracted to *Daily Mirror* again) was turned from failure to success. A few years later, in 1908, Northcliffe bought the ailing *Times* at a time when it was in danger of

Right:
THE DAILY MIRROR
No. 1
November 2, 1903
(415 x 287mm)
The first modern attempt at a
publishing a daily, 'by women
for women' and a failure:
revamped as a popular
illustrated newspaper, a
resounding success.

Below:
DAILY HERALD
No. 2488/1495
January 23, 1924
(575 x 405mm)
Started in 1911 as a Labour
Party strike newssheet, perhaps
its greatest headline announced
the first Labour Government of
1924.

DAILY SKETCH, THURSDAY, JUNE 14, 1917.

HEAVY DEATH ROLL IN LONDON AIR RAID.

DAILY SKETCH.

THE PREMIER PICTURE PAPER.

No. 2,578.   Telegrams: London Holborn 801 Manchester City 4401   LONDON, THURSDAY, JUNE 14, 1917.   (Registered as a Newspaper)   ONE PENNY.

THE KING VISITS AIR RAID VICTIMS.

GOOD MORNING! YES, IT'S TIME FOR A NEW NEWSPAPER

TUESDAY

SUN

SEPTEMBER 15 1964   THREEPENCE   No. 1

THE INDEPENDENT DAILY NEWSPAPER

Election race is on

By TREVOR WILLIAMS, Political Reporter

THEY'RE OFF in the General Election stakes. Today the starting tape goes up for 1,600 men and women in the race for 630 seats in the next House of Commons.

The election date will be made known officially at about 4 pm. today from 10, Downing Street. October 15 can be regarded as a certainty.

Sir Alec Douglas-Home flew to Balmoral last night and will have an audience there with the Queen this morning. Then he will fly back to London to make the long-awaited announcement.

Parliament is expected to be dissolved by Royal

THE British public believe it is time for a new newspaper, born of the age we live in. That is why the SUN rises brightly today.

Here it is—Number One issue of the first new popular daily in this country for 34 years.

What does this newspaper stand for? What is its hope of purpose? What is it all about?

★ The Sun is politically free. It will not automatically support or censure any party or any Government.

★ It is an independent paper designed to serve and inform all those whose lives are changing, improving, expanding in these hurrying years.

★ We welcome the age of automation, electronics, computers. We will campaign for the rapid modernisation of Britain—regardless of the vested interests of managements or workers. But we will crusade against any Government which drives the evolution forward without farsighted schemes for retraining and generous compensation where unemployment arises.

★ The Sun is a newspaper with a social conscience. A radical paper, ready to praise or criticise without preconceived bias. Championing progressive ideas. Fighting injustice. Exposing cruelty and exploitation.

★ Above all, the Sun is a gay—as well as informative—paper for those with a zest for living.

Today's weather
.. see Page Two

going bankrupt. The circulation was increased by tenfold to 30,000.

By the Great War, 1914-1918, most of today's newspapers had taken root. The *Sketch* (eventually amalgamated with the *Mail* in 1971) started in 1909. The *Daily Herald*, forerunner of the *Sun*, began life as a Labour Party strike newssheet in 1911. The *Sunday Pictorial* (the *Sunday Mirror* from 1963) began in 1915, and the Glasgow *Post* in 1914.

Northcliffe was the first of the newspaper barons, but several more emerged during the inter-war period. By 1937 they headed five business groups which controlled most of the national newspapers: Harmsworth, Berry, Cadbury, Beaverbrook and Odhams Press (under Lord Southwood). Lord Beaverbrook was the most flamboyant.

He acquired the *Daily Express* in 1917, founded the *Sunday Express* in 1918, and acquired the London *Evening Standard*, first published in 1860, in 1923.

Newspapers fought hard in the circulation battles of the 1920s. Some did it by offering free gifts and free insurance. The *Herald* achieved two million customers, the first paper in the world to do so, but by the 1930s the newspaper industry was, like everything else, in a state of slump. Even the *Daily Mirror*, the working class tabloid, was down to 700,000 circulation in 1934. Against the trend, the well-established, solidly middle-class *Daily Telegraph*, owned by Lord Camrose, increased its circulation from 100,000 in 1927 to 750,000 in 1939. In political terms *The Times* maintained an influence in the country far beyond that which could be expected from its limited sale. Under the editorship of Geoffrey Dawson, who had the ear of Prime Minister Stanley Baldwin, it became almost an instrument of government policy; its role in the Abdication Crisis of 1936 was an excellent example of this. The late 1930s also saw·the rise of the weekly news and picture magazines such as *Illustrated* and *Picture Post*.

Opposite:
DAILY SKETCH
No. 2578
June 14, 1917
(380 x 315mm)
The Great War boosted the demand for the popular illustrated tabloids such as the Daily Sketch *and* Daily Mirror.

SUN
No. 1
September 15, 1964
(530 x 410mm)
An attempt to bright up the ailing Daily Herald.

During the Second World War, the competing newspaper groups, like other areas of the economy, put their differences to one side in favour of the national effort. They were restricted in size; tabloids to eight pages and broadsheets to four.

After the war, the process of newspaper amalgamations and take-overs continued, despite a number of Royal Commissions into the working of the press. Television, which had disappeared during the war, seemed to be a prime reason for the slow death of the news magazines and a steady decline in newspaper circulation.

Among the newspapers that have disappeared have been the *News Chronicle* (a descendant of the *Daily News*) and the London *Star* in 1960, the *Herald* in 1964, the *Daily Sketch* (amalgamated with the *Daily Mail*) in 1971, the *Sunday Citizen* (founded in 1850 as *Reynolds Weekly Newspaper*) in 1967, the *Sunday Graphic* (founded 1915 as the *Ilustrated Sunday Herald*) and the *Sunday Dispatch* in 1961, and the *Evening News* (taken over by the *Evening Standard*) in 1980.

On the positive side, the *Sunday Telegraph* was launched in 1961 as a stable-mate for the *Daily Telegraph*, the *Sun*, completely revamped from the paper of the same name that had continued where the *Herald* had left off, in 1969, the *Daily Star* 1978 and the *Mail on Sunday* in 1982.

In 1972, three-quarters of British dailies were owned by five business groups: Associated Newspapers, Beaverbrook Newspapers, IPC Daily Mirror Group, United Newspaper Publications and the Thomson Organisation. The total sale of national newspapers in that year totalled 36 million; ten years later it had declined to 32 million. The dominant newspaper groups in 1982 were Fleet Holdings, descendant of Beaverbrook Newspapers and publisher of the *Daily Express*, *Daily Star* and the *Sunday Express*; Associated Newspapers Group, publisher of the *Daily Mail* and *Mail on Sunday*; Reed International, descendant of IPC and publisher of the *Daily Mirror*,

THE SUN, No. 1, November 17, 1969 (376 x 296mm)
The second Sun — Rupert Murdoch's imitation of the Daily Mirror.

*THE SUNDAY
TELEGRAPH
No. 1
February 5, 1961
(600 x 440mm)
A successful new post-war
Sunday newspaper.*

THE
SUNDAY TELEGRAPH
AND ITS AIMS

TODAY appears the first new national Sunday paper for 40 years.

It is not its aim to improve upon some other paper. Instead it is being started in the belief that for educated people there is a sizeable gap in Sunday reading.

THE SUNDAY TELEGRAPH *hopes to fill that gap.*

On one side are two serious and voluminous newspapers whose emphasis is on magazine features; on the other are a larger number which in varying degree tend towards triviality and sensationalism.

THE SUNDAY TELEGRAPH *will not neglect the wider range of reading for which the public has time at the week-end. While deliberately restricting its paging to a manageable size, it will also give a larger proportion of its space than other Sundays to succinct reporting and explanation of news, home and foreign.*

To readers from one side of the gap THE SUNDAY TELEGRAPH will represent " the paper you can finish," and, to those from the other side, it will strive to be " the paper that will satisfy."

READERS of THE DAILY TELEGRAPH will find the format of the Sunday not unfamiliar. To provide a wide variety on Page One, news is carried over where necessary to the back. The rest of the news begins in the centre spread and is continued in consecutive pages. All the main articles are brought together in the front of the paper while sport and classified advertising are moved to the end.

THE SUNDAY TELEGRAPH, *however, is not merely the seventh day edition of* THE DAILY TELEGRAPH. *In a newspaper designed for Sunday a different emphasis is appropriate. A more detailed image of the new paper is contained in a " Letter from the Editor," on Page 8.*

Sunday Mirror and *Sunday People*; and News International (proprietor Rupert Murdoch) publisher of the *Sun* and *The Times, News of the World* and *Sunday Times.*

Despite the decline in sales, more newspapers are sold in Britain, per capita, than most other western countries; three out of four adults over 15 read a national morning paper, one in two an evening paper. And despite the concentration of ownership of most of the national and local newspapers in the hands of a small number of companies, there remains a vigorous competition for readership. Rupert Murdoch's intervention in the newspaper business has had a dramatic effect on content and pattern of sales. Under his ownership the *Sun* and *News of the World* have fought hard for the popular readership offering "page three nudes" and other un-newsworthy attractions, and gaining an imitator in the shape of the *Daily Star*. The *Daily Mirror*, for long the biggest selling daily, now takes second place to the *Sun*.

The biggest change in local papers has been the growth of the "free sheet", give-away papers delivered to every house in the area. Since 1965 the number has risen to over 500. The best of these actually have an editorial content — up to 40% of the total space, but the majority are almost entirely advertising.

Local papers are taking advantage of the new technology, available through computerisation, enabling one journalist-typesetter to write stories, lay out advertising and make up a page all on one visual display unit.

The battle of Fleet Street is between the proprietors and the unions to replace traditional methods with the new technology. The unions do not like it because the change will mean loss of jobs, and the traditional power and high wages of printers are threatened. New technology will come: when and how is still the question.

BRITISH NEWSPAPERS OF THE TWENTIETH CENTURY

I. DAILIES

Name	Controlling company	Average circulation April-September 1983

DAILY EXPRESS Fleet Holdings. 1,936,290. April 1900-

DAILY HERALD
Daily Herald January 1911-September 1914
(Not published April 1911-April 1912)
The Herald October 1914-March 1919
Daily Herald March 1919-September 1964
Renamed *The Sun* September 1964

DAILY MAIL Associated Newspaper Group. 1,820,094. May 1896-

DAILY MIRROR Reed International. 3,419,190. November 1903-January 1904.
Daily Illustrated Mirror January 1904-April 1904
Daily Mirror April 1904-

DAILY RECORD (Scotland). Reed International. 743,528. (January-June 1983.)
Daily Record October 1895-June 1901
Daily Record and Daily Mail June 1901-March 1902
Daily Record and Mail March 1901-March 1954
Daily Record March 1954-

DAILY SKETCH
March 1909-June 1946 (incorporating *Daily Graphic* January 1890-October 1926)
Sketch and Graphic 3 June-29 June 1946
Graphic and Sketch July 1946-January 1953
Sketch and Graphic January 1953-September 1954
Daily Sketch September 1954-May 1971
Incorporated with *Daily Mail* May 1971

DAILY STAR Fleet Holdings. 1,386,256. November 1978-

DAILY TELEGRAPH Telegraph Newspaper Trust. 1,260,932
Daily Telegraph and Courier June 1855-October 1856
Daily Telegraph October 1856-September 1937

Daily Telegraph and Morning Post (incorporating the *Morning Post* October 1937-October 1969

Daily Telegraph October 1969-

EVENING NEWS

July 1881-May 1889

Evening News and Post May 1889-September 1894

Evening News September 1894-August 1901

Evening News and Evening Mail August 1901-March 1905

Evening News March 1905-1980 (incorporated with the *Evening Standard*)

FINANCIAL TIMES Pearson Longman. 212,463.

London Financial Guide January-February 1888

Financial Times February 1888-

GUARDIAN Guardian and Manchester Evening News. 438,464.

Manchester Guardian May 1821-August 1959

The Guardian August 1959-

MORNING STAR People's Press Printing Society c. 30,000 (uncertified).

Daily Worker January 1930-April 1966 (suppressed by Government Jan. 1941-September 1942)

Morning Star April 1966-

NEWS CHRONICLE

Daily News January 1846-May 1912

Daily News and Leader May 1912-January 1928

Daily News and Westminster Gazette February 1928-May 1930

News Chronicle (incorporating *Daily Chronicle* November 1872-May 1930)

News Chronicle June 1930-November 1955

News Chronicle and Daily Dispatch November 1955-October 1960

Incorporated with the *Daily Mail* October 1960

SCOTSMAN 83,984. (January-June 1983).
>
> *Daily Scotsman* July 1855-December 1859
> *Scotsman* January 1860-

THE STANDARD
>
> First published as the evening edition of *The Standard* June 1860-March 1905
> *Evening Standard and St. James's Gazette* March 1905-October 1916
> *Evening Standard* October 1916-1980
> *The Standard* 1980- (incorporating the *Evening News*)

STAR
>
> January 1888-May 1915
> *Star and Echo* May-August 1915
> *Star* August 1915-October 1960
> Incorporated with the *Evening News* October 1960

SUN News International. 4,165,193. September 1964-

THE TIMES News International. 354,071.
>
> *Daily Universal Register* January 1785-December 1787
> *The Times, Or Daily Universal Register* January-March 1788
> *The Times* March 1788-

II. SUNDAYS

EMPIRE NEWS

The Umpire May 1884-March 1917
The Empire April-July 1917
Empire News July 1917-November 1944
Sunday Empire News December 1944-October 1950
Empire News and the Umpire 8-22 October 1950
Empire News October 1950-November 1955
Empire News and Sunday Chronicle November 1955-October 1960 (incorporating *Sunday Chronicle* founded August 1855) Incorporated with *News of the World* October 1960

MAIL ON SUNDAY Associated Newspaper Group. 1,372,671. May 1982-

NEWS OF THE WORLD News International. 4,041,888. October 1843-.

OBSERVER George Outram and Co., subsidiary of Longman. 767,725. December 1791-.

SUNDAY CITIZEN

Reynold's Weekly Newspaper May 1850-February 1851
Reynold's Newspaper February 1851-Feburary 1923
Reynold's News March 1923-September 1924
Reynold's Illustrated News September 1924-February 1936
Reynold's News March 1936-August 1944
Reynold's News and Sunday Citizen August 1944-62
Sunday Citizen September 1962-January 1967

SUNDAY DISPATCH

Weekly Dispatch September 1801-June 1928
Sunday Dispatch July 1928-June 1961

SUNDAY EXPRESS Fleet Holdings. 2,610,996. December 1918-

Illustrated Sunday Herald March 1915-May 1927

Sunday Herald and Sunday Graphic May-September 1927 (incorporating *Sunday Graphic*, February 1920-October 1926)

Sunday Graphic and Sunday Herald September 1927-April 1929

Sunday Graphic April 1929-December 1960

SUNDAY MIRROR Reed International. 3,623,420.

Sunday Pictorial March 1915-March 1963

Sunday Mirror and Pictorial April-June 1963

Sunday Mirror July 1963-

SUNDAY PEOPLE Reed International. 3,492,769.

The People October 1881-December 1971

Sunday People January 1972-

SUNDAY POST D. C. Thomson. Over 1,000,000.

The Post Glasgow October 1914-January 1919

Sunday Post January 1919-

SUNDAY TIMES News International. 1,278,820.

New Observer February-March 1821

Independent Observer April 1821-October 1822

Sunday Times October 1822-

A GUIDE TO COLLECTING

THE SURVIVAL FACTOR

Examples of nearly all of the newspapers mentioned in the preceding brief history of the British press can be found by anyone seriously making an effort to collect them, despite their obviously ephemeral nature.

This means, in practice, that today's newspaper collector may well be able to find *an* issue or longer run of any periodical, but find it impossible to obtain a *particular* issue or run.

There are, of course, thousands more newspapers that would have to be mentioned in a comprehensive history. Many of these will be just as commonly found as those named, but many others, particularly in the earliest period have not survived at all or can only be seen as odd copies or broken runs in the major libraries.

The scope for collecting is greatest in the modern period, dating from about 1800, though it is true to say that several of the longer lasting eighteenth-century newspapers will be commonly encountered, while unstamped papers of the 1830s for instance are of great scarcity. Prior to 1800, even the major dailies were only printed in hundreds of copies. The possibility of acquiring examples is still high, but it is getting more difficult to find them in quantity or in runs extending over several years.

Most of these early newspapers that have survived, were originally bound up into volume form. Individual copies found today still bear signs in the left hand margin of the tell-tale "stab-marks" made by the binder when sewing the issues together in half-yearly or yearly runs. Single copies which have survived without being bound up are usually "freaks" or special issues and, without the mutual protection given to each newspaper within a volume, are unlikely to be in good condition. Seventeenth-century newsbooks and Civil War pamphlets are still to be found in volumes at auction and in booksellers' catalogues. The eighteenth-century essay papers, such as the *Spectator* and *Tatler* and Hawkesworth's *Adventurer,* 1752-54, containing many contributions by

Samuel Johnson, were many times reprinted in volume form, though in a smaller format. Copies of the *Gentleman's Magazine,* for instance, are still commonly found in bound volumes, though now often broken up to extract the maps and illustrations which they contained. Individual issues, however, with uncut edges (almost always trimmed when periodicals are bound) and in the original wrappers are scarce.

Through the nineteenth century, the tradition of binding newspapers for gentlemen's libraries continued. *The Times*, as *the* gentleman's newspaper, was commonly given this reverential treatment, so that bound volumes can still be quite readily found today. Of the nineteenth-century weeklies, the *Illustrated London News* is the commonest.

The whole business of "binding up" stemmed from the traditions of bookselling. In the late eighteenth century when books were beginning to reach a wider audience, they were generally bound initially only in flimsy paper wrappers or card boards. The edges of the pages were left uncut. The publisher might well have a certain number done up in a leather binding, but for the most part it was left to the purchaser either to read the book in its published state, which was quite possible by just slitting the unopened pages, or if the purchaser was wealthy enough to want his library shelves filled with leather-bound tomes he would pay his bookseller to have them bound.

The link between newspaper and books in this respect was forged by the "part publications" of the late eighteenth to mid-nineteenth centuries. These were essentially books, but published in magazine form, one part every week or month over a period of a year or so. Thomas Rowlandson, the caricaturist, published his famous series of engravings of Dr Syntax in this way (1812-1821) with accompanying "letter-press" or text, linking the engravings. Charles Dickens, a journalist with the *Mirror of Parliament, Morning Chronicle, True Sun* and later editor of several literary journals and (for a few initial weeks) the *Daily News,* changed the emphasis of the "part work". Before Dickens, the pictures had been the main reason for purchase, but with the publication of his *Pickwick Papers* in 1837, it was the text the public wanted to read. This, and most of his subsequent novels, were published in twenty monthly parts designed at the conclusion to be bound in book form.

The publishers of many newspapers and periodicals also offered binding services to their readers; usually a new general title page would be supplied together with an index and contents page. With increasing numbers of pages per volume, and increased page size, it became a rather expensive business.

While *The Times* ruled supreme in the newspaper world, it was the *one* paper above all the others that was regarded as respectable, responsible and reliable and, therefore, the one to be bound up as an excellent source of reference. The lesser papers, with lower circulations and especially those more cheaply produced for the working man, had much less chance of being bound, and therefore of surviving. Comparison with literary part-works reinforces the picture: works by the major authors such as Dickens and Thackeray have survived quite extensively in parts; novels by minor authors are virtually impossible to find.

Into the twentieth century, although periodicals have continued to be bound for reference, very few people have continued to have their newspapers preserved in a binding. Occasionally libraries, or even newspapers themselves, sell off runs which have been bound up, but newspapers of the twentieth century depend greatly on owners, with large houses, keeping them in store, unbound. Because of the appeals from government during the Second World War to recycle "waste paper", the survival rate of 1920s and 1930s papers is very low. Postwar, enormous quantities have found homes in attics, basements and spare rooms.

APPROACHES TO COLLECTING

I. NEWSPAPER HISTORY — AN INITIAL APPROACH

A perspective across history of the development of newspapers, as outlined in the first part of this book, is perhaps the simplest and most appropriate suggestion as the first collecting theme. This involves the acquisition of a variety of newspapers over a specific short period, a century, or a representative sample from the seventeenth century to the present time.

Such an approach has infinite possibilities for expansion, and at the same time provides a broad base from which any future specialisation can grow. It concentrates more on the changes in newspapers themselves rather than on the information carried in them; first issues, important dates in history or headlines are not essential.

As a result, the cost of building up such a collection will be relatively low. Generally speaking, prices will increase the older the newspaper. English "Mercuries" of the Civil War period, like most papers up to the beginning of the nineteenth century, were printed in hundreds rather than thousands. Modern newspapers, printed in hundreds of thousands, are obviously more common. Second World War papers, without a striking headline, will cost pence rather than pounds. The biggest problem in the period after about 1860 is finding good condition examples. Mass production has meant much poorer quality newsprint, easily browned, easily becoming brittle.

II. HISTORY IN NEWSPAPERS —

SCOOP, SCANDAL AND STRIFE

"Headlines" sums up the second, and probably the most popular, approach to newspaper collecting. Concentrating on the content, rather than the development, make-up and style of the newspapers themselves, it is the scoops and major news of history that are at the heart of the matter.

Headlines as such started to appear towards the end of the nineteenth century. Before then, barring exceptional events such as coronations and deaths of monarchs, the most important affairs of state shared equal, very undistinguished, billing with the most boring of law reports or garden parties.

"Headlines" approach can be divided into: (a) a particular "period" of history — the Second World War for instance; (b) "type" of news reported — air crashes, earthquakes, space travel; (c) "place" of publication — newspapers from the place from where the news came — Unilateral Declaration of Independence by white Rhodesians under Mr Ian Smith on 11 November 1965 as reported in the next day's *Rhodesia Herald:* "UDI RHODESIA GOES IT ALONE", for instance. (An issue interesting for what is not printed — large gaps were left where government censors refused to allow publication of articles.) When the first men landed on the moon in July 1969, the ideal *Lunar News* was not available; second best is the *Wapakoneta Daily News,* from Wapakoneta, Ohio, home of Neil A. Armstrong, headed NEIL STEPS ON THE MOON on 21 July, the ultimate "local boy makes good" story. Such geographical accuracy in getting the report from the place nearest to the event means keeping close contact with other collectors around the world, or writing to the local paper.

Headlines from the places making the news.

Top: *THE RHODESIA HERALD, November 12, 1965 (580 x 470mm)*

Below: *WAPAKONETA DAILY NEWS, No., 65-14, July 21, 1969 (570 x 405mm)*

IMPENDING RESIGNATION

OF

MR. GLADSTONE.

GRAVE POLITICAL CRISIS.

DISSOLUTION PROBABLE.

We have reason to know, from an authority which we are not able to disclose, but in which we have every confidence, that Mr. Gladstone has finally decided to resign office almost immediately. We understand that the letter announcing his resolution will be sent to the Queen before the reassembling of Parliament. This decision is due to a sense of his advanced age and to the great strain of the late arduous session. He is also deeply disappointed at the rejection of the Home Rule Bill, and at the opposition which the Parish Councils Bill has encountered. Domestic pressure, moreover, has not been without considerable influence in determining his mind at last. Who will succeed him ? And what will be the result ?

Opposite:
THE EVENING NEWS
No. 25258
March 22, 1963
(590 x 412mm)

DAILY EXPRESS
No. 19600
June 6, 1963
(600 x 410mm)
The Profumo Scandal. Initial
bluff and final resignation.

A 'stop-press' headline for the normally staid PALL MALL GAZETTE, January 31, 1894.

MERCURIUS RUSTICUS
Title page of the first collected
edition of this English Civil
War Newsbook, 1647

WARS, AND RUMOURS OF WARS

"War takes first place among the causes of the newspaper" wrote Stanley Morison, typographer and newspaper historian. Wars have provided more headlines than any other human activity.

In Britain, the Civil War 1642-1651, gave impetus to the development of a free press, even though it was officially supposed to be strictly licensed and controlled. In the 1790s and 1800s, the Napoleonic Wars helped to boost newspaper circulations even though the British government restricted foreign reports in the domestic press. In America, the War of Independence 1770-1782, provided the same sort of impetus to newspapers as the Civil War had done in Britain over a hundred years earlier. Out of it emerged such sensational papers as the *Massachusetts Spy or, American Oracle of Liberty* and the *Boston Gazette*. America's own Civil War 1861-1865 provoked vehement partizanship on both sides which was reflected in the newspapers. It also produced some of the best early war correspondents (although William Russell of *The Times* is acknowledged to be the first for his reports of the Crimea War) and some ingenious answers to paper shortage. The *Daily Citizen* of Vicksburg, Mississippi for 2 July 1863, is printed on wallpaper "for the last time" the reader is informed. The virulence of the content in support of the Confederate cause is worth note:

> The former editors of the *Memphis Bulletin* being rather pro-Southern were arrested for speaking the truth when truth was unwelcome to Yankee-dom. This paper at present is . . . edited by a pink-nosed, slab-sided, toad-eating Yankee, who is a lineal descendant of Judas Iscariot, and a brother germain of the greatest Puritanical, sycophantic, howling scoundrel unhung — Parson Brownlow.

Good newes from *Fraunce.*

A true Discourse of

the winning of sundry cheefe Townes,
Castles, and holdes in *Fraunce*, which
are now in the obedience of the
French King.

With the great Victorie which
his Maieslie hath had in sundry late Battels,
Skirmishes, and pursuites made vpon the
enemy at *Mouncounter* in *Brittanie,* and
else where, since the winning of
*Chartres,*which was in
Aprill laſt.

Together with the defeating, drow-
ning, and taking of much victuaile, corne,
and mony sent by the Enemy to the
Cittie of Paris.

Published by Authoritie.

AT LONDON
Printed for Thomas Nelſon,
and are to be ſolde by William
Wright.

OCTOBER 25.

If the exhibition of the most brilliant valour, of the excess of courage, and of a daring which would have reflected lustre on the best days of chivalry can afford full consolation for the disaster of to-day, we can have no reason to regret the melancholy loss which we sustained in a contest with a savage and barbarian enemy.

I shall proceed to describe, to the best of my power, what occurred under my own eyes, and to state the facts which I have heard from men whose veracity is unimpeachable, reserving to myself the exercise of the right of private judgment in making public and in suppressing the details of what occurred on this memorable day. Before I proceed to my narrative, I must premise that a certain feeling existed in some quarters that our cavalry had not been properly handled since they landed in the Crimea, and that they had lost golden opportunities from the indecision and excessive caution of their leaders. It was said that our cavalry ought to have been manœuvred at Bouljanak in one way or in another, according to the fancy of the critic. It was affirmed, too, that the light cavalry were utterly useless in the performance of one of their most important duties—the collection of supplies for the army—that they were "above their business, and too fine gentlemen for their work;" that our horse should have pushed on after the flying enemy after the battle of the Alma, to their utter confusion, and with the certainty of taking many guns and prisoners; and, above all, that at Mackenzie's-farm first, and at the gorge near Inkermann subsequently, they had been improperly restrained from charging, and had failed in gaining great successes, which would have entitled them to a full share of the laurels of the campaign, solely owing to the timidity of the officer in command. The existence of this feeling was known to many of our cavalry, and they were indignant and exasperated that the faintest shade of suspicion should rest on any of their corps. With the justice of these aspersions they seemed to think they had nothing to do, and perhaps the prominent thought in their minds was that they would give such an example of courage to the world, if the chance offered itself, as would shame their detractors for ever.

Opposite:
GOOD NEWES FROM
FRAUNCE
(175 x 135mm)
1591
Supposedly issued by the
French Embassy to give
publicity in England for the
successes achieved by the King
of France.

Right:
THE TIMES
No. 21, 898
November 14, 1854
The Charge of the Light
Brigade as reported by W. C.
Russell, the first war
correspondent.

THE DAILY CITIZEN.

J. M. SWORDS,......Proprietor.

VICKSBURG, MISS.

THURSDAY, JULY 2, 1863.

☛Mrs. Cisco was instantly killed on Monday, on the Jackson road. Mrs. Cisco's husband is now in Virginia, a member of Moody's Artillery, and the death of such a loving, affectionate, and dutiful wife will be a loss to him irreparable.

☛We are indebted to Major Gillespie for a steak of Confederate beef, *alias* meat. We have tried it, and can assure our friends that if it is rendered necessary, they need have no scruples at eating the meat. It is sweet, savory, and tender, and so long as we have a mule left we are satisfied our soldiers will be content to subsist on it.

☛Jerre Askew, one of our most esteemed merchant-citizens, was wounded at the works in the rear of our city a few days since, and breathed his last on Monday. Mr. Askew was a young man of strict integrity, great industry and an honor to his family and friends. He was a member of Cowan's artillery, and by the strict discharge of his duties and his obliging disposition, won the confidence and esteem of his entire command. May the blow his family have sustained be mitigated by Him who doeth all things well.

☛Grant's forces did a little firing on Tuesday afternoon, but the balance of that day was comparatively quiet. Yesterday morning they were very still, and continued so until early in the afternoon, when they sprung a mine on the left of our center, and opened fire along the line for some distance. We have not been able to ascertain anything definitely as to our loss, but as our officers were on the lookout for this move of the enemy, the expectations of the Yankees were not realized by a great deal.

☛Among many deeds we hear spo-

GOOD NEWS.—In devoting a large portion of our space this morning to federal intelligence, copied from the Memphis Bulletin of the 25th, it should be remembered that the news in the original truth is whitewashed by the Federal Provost Marshal, who desires to hoodwink the poor Northern white slaves. The former editors of the Bulletin being rather pro-southern men, were arrested for speaking the truth when truth was unwelcome to Yankeedom, and placed in the chain-gang working at Warrenton, where they now are. This paper at present is in duress and edited by a pink-nosed, slab-sided, toad-eating Yankee, who is a lineal descendant of Judas Iscariot, and a brother germain of the greatest Puritanical, sycophantic, howling scoundrel unhung—Parson Brownlow. Yet, with such a character, this paper cannot cloak the fact that Gen. Rob't E. Lee has given Hooker, Milroy & Co, one of the best and soundest whippings on record, and that the "glorious Union" is now exceedingly weak in the knees.

Gen. Rob't E. Lee Again.

Again we have reliable news from the gallant corps of Gen. Lee in Virginia. Elated with success, encouraged by a series of brilliant victories, marching to and crossing the Rappahannock, defeating Hooker's right wing and thence through the Shenandoah valley, driving Milroy from Winchester and capturing 6,000 of his men and a large amount of valuable stores of all descriptions, re-entering Maryland, holding Hagerstown, threatening Washington City, and within a few miles of Baltimore— onward and upward their war cry—our brave men under Lee are striking terror to the hearts of all Yankeedom. Like the Scottish chieftain's clans, Lee's men are springing up from moor and brake, crag and dale, with flashing steel and sturdy arm, ready to do or die in the great cause of national independence, right and honor. To-day the mongrel administration of Lincoln, like Japhet, are in search of a father, for their old Abe has departed to parts unknown. Terror reigns in their halls. Lee is to the left of them, the right of them, in front of them and all around them; and daily do we expect to hear of his being down on them. Never were the French in Algeria more put out by the mobile

108

Above: DAILY EXPRESS, May 19, 1900 (570 x 400mm)
Relief of Mafeking; a minor victory against the Boers makes a banner headline.

Left: THE DAILY CITIZEN of Vicksburg, Mississippi, U.S.A. July 2, 1863 (430 x 250mm)
Just one page printed on floral-patterned wallpaper. Newsprint was clearly a scarce commodity for the Confederates.

DAILY MIRROR, No. 16451, November 1, 1956 (374 x 302mm)
Suez; the Mirror's opinion — 'The attack on Egypt is the culminating blunder in Eden's disastrous Middle East record.'

110

Britain's earliest banner headlines were provoked by incidents in the Boer War of 1898-1901. News of the Relief of Mafeking was broken to the British public by the *Daily Express* with an across-the-page headline for the first time. The Boer War was also important because of the political ripples caused by critical newspaper reporting of the government's handling of the war. Ridicule of long-overdue army reforms even came from the advertisement columns: "Clean up the War Office, Lord Kitchener" demanded the monkey on Monkey Brand soap, and, as the war dragged on, pictures and reports of the exploits of "British heroes" changed to pointed complaints about the army's inability to dispose of Boer farmers outnumbered five to one.

During the Great War 1914-18 news was transmitted around the world within hours by means of radio and telegraph. It was the first war in which photographs were widely employed by newspapers, although censorship kept any real idea of what conditions were like at the Front away from genteel breakfast tables back home. The picture papers, especially the *Daily Mirror* and *Daily Sketch* became widely popular for the first time. It was in the Great War, too, that soldiers' newspapers made a showing: the *Wipers Times* on the Western Front, and the *Balkan News* in the Middle East.

World War II newspapers suffered badly from lack of newsprint. By the war's end broadsheet newspapers were restricted to four pages, and tabloids to eight. All news was censored, Allied setbacks underplayed and successes exaggerated; but front-line correspondents described battles at first hand in greater detail than ever before.

Reporting of the far eastern wars in Korea and, particularly, Vietnam exposed the full impact of war, in words and pictures, to the world's newspaper-reading public. The image of the dead civilian and soldier became commonplace. President Nixon, commenting on the press coverage of

Evening Chronicle

INCORPORATING THE "EVENING WORLD"

EXTRA

1,696 TRAVELLING RUGS
5·11 each.
FARNONS, Nun St.

No. 15,580. [Established 1885] NEWCASTLE, THURSDAY, OCTOBER 3, 1935. PRICE ONE PENNY

Four Meals a Day —
Four Opportunities for
HOE'S
Delicious
SAUCE

WAR BEGUN: ITALIAN 'PLANES IN ACTION
Adowa and Adigrat Bombarded: Hundreds Killed—Official

TROOPS ADVANCE THROUGH
VALLEYS AT DAWN

Mass Attack on Ethiopian Towns
From the Air

VIVID STORY OF OFFENSIVE

Women and Children Killed
by Bombs

WAR BEGAN THIS MORNING

THE ITALIAN ARMIES CROSSED THE ABYSSINIAN FRONTIER AT DAWN AT WIDELY SEPARATED POINTS, CONVERGING TOWARDS ADOWA, AND BOMBING, FIGHTING AND SCOUTING PLANES SET OUT TO BOMB ADIGRAT, ADOWA AND OTHER ETHIOPIAN TOWNS.

The aerial attack of the famous "desperate squadron" was led by Mussolini's son-in-law, Count Ciano, and the Duce's two sons took part.

The Abyssinian Government has sent a Note to the League protesting

1,700 CASUALTIES IN
ADOWA—OFFICIAL

CONSTERNATION IN
LEAGUE CIRCLES

ITALIAN AND ETHIOPIAN
NOTES TO GENEVA

COUNCIL SUMMONED

The Evening News

LATE EXTRA

Gordon's Gin
THE HEART OF A GOOD COCKTAIL
Stands Supreme

La Coquille

LARGEST EVENING NET SALE IN THE WORLD

LONDON, FRIDAY, SEPTEMBER 1, 1939.

BROADCASTING PAGE 4

ONE PENNY

LONDON FORECAST

POLAND INVADED
BRITAIN AND FRANCE MOBILISE
Big German Offensive on the Corridor : Bombing Raids
on Warsaw, Cracow and other Polish Towns

DANZIG ANNEXED BY
PROCLAMATION

Polish Ambassador Invokes The
Treaty And Calls For Aid

HITLER AND ITALY: "I DO NOT APPEAL
TO FOREIGN HELP"

General mobilisation was ordered in Britain and France this afternoon when it became known that Germany had invaded Poland and had bombed many towns, including Warsaw.

The King signed an Order in Council for the mobilisation of the Army and

PARLIAMENT
SUMMONED
FOR 6 P.M.

TERRITORIALS

GERMAN RAIL
STATION SHELLED

On Other Pages

BRITAIN
STANDS BY

19 TUBE STATIONS TO
CLOSE

the Vietnam War, and implying that perhaps censorship might have been the correct course to protect those at home from the atrocities of war, said that bringing the horror of war into every home was "a terrible price to pay" for the freedom of the press. That freedom played its part in bringing the war to an end.

Opposite:
EVENING CHRONICLE
No. 15550
October 3, 1935
(600 x 434mm)
The Italian Invasion of
Ethiopia.

THE EVENING NEWS
No. 17978
(600 x 434mm)
The German Invasion of
Poland — prelude to the
Second World War

Right:
THE DUG-OUT GAZETTE
No. 4
September, 1916
(245 x 155mm)
Entertainment for the Western
Front trenches during the Great
War.

DAILY STAR

FRIDAY, MAY 21st, 1982   14p (15p C.I.s, 18p Eire) Printed in London

FALKLANDS
INVASION
SPECIAL
EDITION

May 20, 1982: The day
the talking stopped

IN WE GO

Admiral Sandy gets the order: Hit them early and hard

THE go-ahead to invade the Falklands was given to Task Force Commander Sandy Woodward last night.

He now has, complete freedom of action to smash the Argentinians' hold on the islands.

The top-level message from Whitehall was: "Hit them early and hit them hard. Do not hang about."

Last night it looked as though

By ANTHONY SMITH
Defence Correspondent

commandos could be ordered ashore within hours.

The momentous political decision made by the War Cabinet means that Britain is at war with Argentina in everything but name.

However, the Foreign Secretary emphasised last night that although shooting may start, diplomacy will continue.

The actual strategy 8,000 miles away in the South Atlantic will be left to Admiral Woodward and his

commanders on the warships now at battle formation off the Falklands.

But he is expected to launch a widely scattered six-pronged attack, mainly concentrated on East Falkland where the Argentinian troops are gathered in strength.

He will not send thousands of Royal Marines and commandos pouring on to the sandy beaches around Port Stanley in the early stages of the assault like a D-Day invasion.

Demoralised

Instead, commando units will first take out the cold and hungry Argentinian encampments which have been set up away from Port Stanley.

Many of these small encampments are occupied by badly trained and young conscript troops who, it is thought, are already demoralised by the barrage of shells fired by warships, and Harriers streaking overhead.

When this outer defensive wing has been neutralised, the British troops will move in to isolate the better trained and more hardened veterans of the Argentinian forces.

The Argentinian garrison on West Falkland will be virtually ignored in the early stages, apart from some strategic shelling to

Turn to Page 2

Special reports on Pages 2, 3, 4, 11, 14 and 15

DAILY STAR, May 21, 1982 (385 x 300mm)

Above: THE BALKAN NEWS, No. 131, March 11, 1917 (480 x 320mm).
More serious news and comment for the British troops in the Balkans.

Below: THE TIMES, No. 57165, February 2, 1968 (600 x 440mm)
Image of a horrific war. And Nixon stands again for President.

THE

ACCOUCHEMENT

OF

HER MAJESTY.

BIRTH OF A PRINCE.

THE TIMES-OFFICE, *Tuesday Morning,*
Half-past 8 o'Clock.

We have the happiness to announce that the Queen has been safely delivered of a PRINCE.

We are happy to state that Her Majesty is doing well.

We are indebted to the extraordinary power of the Electro-Magnetic Telegraph for the rapid communication of this important announcement.

THE TIMES
August 6, 1864
Royal news provided via the
'Electro-Magnetic Telegraph'.

116

THE STRANGE FASCINATION OF ROYALTY

If a newspaper is consciously preserved in the average household, it is usually one of two things: a memento of a personal experience or, more likely, a souvenir of a royal or state occasion.

Print runs for "royal" issues are usually much higher than normal and this, combined with the common belief that they are "worth keeping", means a higher survival rate than for any other category.

The relationship between British monarchs and the press has not always been a happy one. Elizabeth I and James did all they could to suppress the printing and reading of news, while later monarchs, notably George III, have been submitted to merciless lampooning. Not until the reign of Queen Victoria, and the ersatz pomp of the kings and queens of the twentieth century, did the royals become the darlings of the press. Coronations, jubilees, births and deaths are traditionally times when newspapers go to town. The *Sun* produced a "gold" printed issue for Victoria's Coronation in 1838 and for her Diamond Jubilee sixty years later the "Golden *Daily Mail*" had an enormous sale. For the Silver Jubilee of George V and Queen Mary, the *Daily Mail* printed a special issue in black on silver glossy paper.

Deaths have traditionally been recorded by special issues with black borders. A striking example of this, for a political rather than a royal leader, is the *New York Herald's* edition for 15 April 1865 reporting the assassination of President Lincoln. Winston Churchill received equal "royal" coverage on his death a century later in 1965.

The birth of Queen Victoria's second son on 6 August 1844 had a special significance for the press: news of the Great Event was conveyed by Electric Telegraph. Princess Elizabeth's marriage to the Duke of Edinburgh received extra-special attention in 1947. It was the first spectacular celebration after the War in the middle of a period of strict austerity and the newspapers took full advantage of it.

HEREFORD TIMES
December 28, 1861
(640 x 450mm)

EVENING NEWS
January 22, 1901
(600 x 430mm)
The deaths of Queen and
Consort; the reports, like the
funeral invitations, edged with
black.

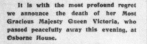

Of all royal events, the Abdication of King Edward VIII in 1936 and Queen Elizabeth's Coronation in 1953 were the two which had important repercussions for the press.

During the Abdication Crisis, British newspapers, led by *The Times* under Geoffrey Dawson, held back from reporting to the public what was happening between King Edward and Mrs Simpson for fear of adversely affecting the situation. Meanwhile the American press had no such scruples and carried every scrap of scandal about the couple. When Britons knew little or nothing of the crisis, citizens of Baltimore could read in the *Baltimore Sun* "MRS SIMPSON, KING'S FRIEND, ASKS FOR DIVORCE". A *Chicago Tribune* cartoon pictured "Cinderella Up to Date" with Edward fitting the glass slipper on Mrs Simpson's foot. Edward cries "It fits! It fits!! At last I've found you!" while Henry VIII looks down from the wall

NORTHERN DESPATCH
No. 6756
December 10, 1936
(600 x 428mm)
Departure of the Uncrowned King, boldly headlined. Edward VIII's affair with Mrs Simpson was, however, kept from the front pages by the British press until only a few days before the Act of Abdication.

119

DAILY EXPRESS
June 3, 1953
(590 x 460mm)
A Queen is crowned — and the
Express *acknowledges the*
superiority of a new rival

THE SUN
January 14, 1983
(370 x 300mm)
The other face of royal
reporting: Invasion of privacy
by press photographers or
Princess Diana acting 'like a
spoilt brat'?

120

muttering "A mere amateur" and British journalists peep from behind a pillar, "The biggest news story in the world and I've got to . . . Sh-h-h". The *New York Daily News* target for abuse from England for its mud-slinging, accurately assessed the problem with British newspaper proprietors: "Most of them think of themselves as statesmen first and publishers second, a long way second". Abdication was almost a fact before the British public knew anything about it. A mere five days before the Act of Abdication, the *Daily Mirror* finally asked Prime Minister Baldwin: "TELL US THE FACTS".

The 1953 Coronation marked a turning point for the British press: as the *Express* headlined it, "QUEEN'S DAY, T.V.'S DAY". A new medium was, for the first time, regarded as superior to the newspaper for providing coverage of a great national event, and the newspapers themselves were the first to admit it.

Of all the themes for collecting newspapers, royalty is the easiest: big special editions are usually widely distributed.

DAILY MAIL, Continental Edition, No. 11654, October 29, 1929 (620 x 430mm).
Wall Street Crash.

THE STAR OF CHILE, No. 105, August 25, 1906 (510 x 384mm).
The Earthquake that also destroyed San Francisco.

EVENING STANDARD, No. 44594, November 6, 1967 (410 x 318mm).
Hither Green rail crash.

DISASTERS

Great human disasters are the oysters of the newspaper world in which are sometimes found the pearl of a scoop, an exclusive report beating the opposition into print.

A disaster is always a strong test for a newspaper. It brings out the best in a good paper or shows a bad paper up for what it is: air crashes like the R101 airship 1930, sunken ships such as the Titanic in April 1912 or the Lusitania torpedoed by enemy action in 1915, natural disasters like the San Francisco Earthquake of 1906. The *Star of Chile*, an English language newspaper, also published in 1906, carried the following note to readers on the front page of its 25 August edition:

> Owing to the want of either electric or gas power we are unable to publish in our usual form. A further difficulty has been experienced by the Propietary *(sic)* in obtaining compositors willing to stand at their posts in view of the recurring earth tremors. We are therefore compelled to issue a four-page special number which contains an account of the catastrophe from the first shock on the night of the 16th inst. to the present date.

The Saturday 11 December 1965 issue of the *Matlock Mercury* filled the front page with:

> FLOOD ISSUE: Standing waist-high in filthy water, we yesterday salvaged twelve pages of your *Mercury*. Uncorrected and incomplete, it's the best we could turn out in the circumstances. Next week's issue will contain full flood reports and pictures — I hope! EDITOR

As Arthur Christiansen, the night editor on the *Sunday Express* when the R101 crashed, said: "It was like being an editor in an American movie." The world is never short of disasters, it seems, and newspaper reporters are always there.

MATLOCK MERCURY
No. 1722
December 11, 1965
(472 x 310mm)
Waist high in water, but the
presses keep rolling.

GODFREY WINN'S QUESTION—TO YOU! Page 11

Daily Mirror

THE DAILY PICTURE   NEWSPAPER WITH THE LARGEST NET SALE

TUESDAY
Dec. 1. No. 10297
ONE PENNY

Registered at the G.P.O. as a newspaper.

QUIET CORNER - Page 27	CASSANDRA - - - - 14	STARS' MESSAGE - - 25	AMUSEMENTS - - - 20	BROADCASTING - - - 18
BELINDA - - - - 26	RUGGLES - - - - 29	SERIAL STORY - - 22	GORDON FIFE - - - 22	PIP & SQUEAK - - 20

FIRE WRECKS CRYSTAL PALACE: ROYAL DUKE WATCHES

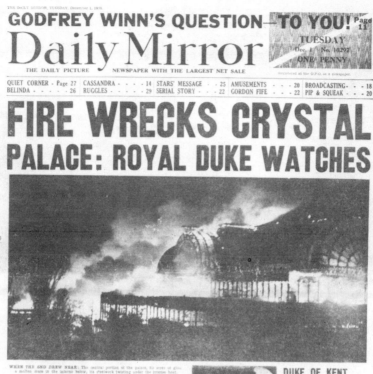

WHEN THE END DREW NEAR: The central portion of the palace, its acres of glass a molten mass in the inferno below, its steelwork twisting under the intense heat.

WITH FLAMES RISING TO A HEIGHT OF 500 FEET, STREAMS OF MOLTEN GLASS FORCING BACK FIREMEN AND SPARKS BEING HURLED THREE MILES, THE CRYSTAL PALACE, LONDON'S WORLD-FAMOUS £2,000,000 ALL-GLASS EXHIBITION BUILDING, WAS DESTROYED LAST NIGHT ONLY ITS TWO 282-FOOT TOWERS WERE LEFT STANDING.

MILLIONS watched the fire. It could be seen in Brighton, fifty miles away. An air liner pilot in mid-Channel, eighty miles away, sighted the glare. At midnight two-thirds of the building was in ruins. The fire was then under control.

Thousands raced from scores of surrounding towns and villages to see the spectacle. For three miles around roads were completely blocked by cars. Many fire engines found it impossible to get within half a mile.

In their news bulletin the B.B.C. advised crowds not to go too near because of the difficulties that faced the police.

Ninety engines were on the spot with 480 firemen. The entire London Fire Brigade was mobilised and every machine stood by.

The tremendous heat could be felt half a mile away. Firemen were unable to work near the flames for more than a minute. Several were injured and taken away.

The noise as the roof crashed could be heard for miles away.

Police cars raced through the thronged streets calling through their loudspeakers for

[Continued on back page]

The Duke of Kent chatting with Mr. Morris, chief of London Fire Brigade.

DUKE OF KENT WEARS A FIREMAN'S HELMET

THE Duke of Kent, in evening dress, arrived by car shortly before midnight and chatted to the firemen who took him off to the smouldering ruins.

At 2 a.m. he was still there—wearing gum boots and a fireman's helmet.

A cascade of water from a fire hose fell over the Duke. He retreated, still smiling, to have a cup of coffee at a brigade motor canteen which had just arrived.

He stood at the counter surrounded by firemen.

After his coffee, which the Duke had at 1.15 a.m., he went with the chief of the London Fire Brigade in a staff car for a tour round the glowing wreckage to see for himself the extent of the havoc.

Then he visited the fire brigade intelligence headquarters, which had been established in a waiting room at Crystal Palace Station.

There he saw firemen and gas engineers busy with maps, working out the positions of the various mains, and directing parties of workmen who had been rushed from London to go and turn off the gas.

DAILY MIRROR, December 1, 1936 (380 x 300mm)
The Gutting of the Crystal Palace by fire.

"BLOODY MURDER" AND OTHER CRIMES

"Three Bloodie Murders" headlined a news pamphlet of 1613. Its front-page woodcut showed an assailant hacking at the body of his victim, one leg already cut asunder, discovered in the act by a "dombe mayde". The sensational formula — guarantee of a good sale — remains exactly the same to the present day.

Crime in broadsides and balladsheets developed into the staple diet of popular nineteenth-century journals, usually published on Sundays, such as the *Observer, Sunday Times* and *News of the World*. As an example, the *Observer* for 8 January 1832 (price 7d): the front page was taken over by a trial report from the Old Bailey following the murder of Margaret Duffy. Other criminal activities were reported under the heading "Robberies and Other Depredations", and apart from "extraordinary occurrences" such as "explosions of gas in the Strand" and the story

Three Bloodie Murders

The firft, committed by *Francis Cartwright* vpon *William Storre.* M Art, Miniſter and Preacher at *Market Raiſin* in the countie of *Lincolne*.

The Second, committed by *Elizabeth Iames*, on the body of her Mayde, in Pariſh of *Egham* in *Surrie*: who was condemned for the fame faЄt at Saint Margarets hill in Southwark, the 2. of Iuly 1613. and lieth in the White Lion till her deliuerie: difcouered by a dombe Mayde, and a Dogge.

The Third, committed vpon a Stranger, very lately neere *High-gate* foure mil from *London*: very ſtrangely found out by a Dogge alfo, the 2. of Iuly, 1613

A rare illustrated newsbook from 1613.

POLICE GAZETTE; OR, HUE AND CRY.

Published by Authority.

No. 447.] SATURDAY, APRIL 28, 1832.

Containing the Substance of all Informations received in Cases of Felonies, and Misdemeanors of an aggravated nature, and against Receivers of Stolen Goods, reputed Thieves and Offenders escaped from Custody, with the time, the place, and every particular circumstance marking the Offence. The Names of Persons charged, who are known but not in Custody, and of those who are not known, their Appearance, Dress, and every other mark of identity that can be described. The Names of Accomplices and Accessories, with every other particular which may lead to their Apprehension. The Names of all Persons brought before the Magistrates, charged with any of the Offences mentioned, and whether committed for Trial, Re-examination, or how otherwise disposed of. Also a Description of Property that has been Stolen, and particularly of Stolen Horses, with as much particularity as can be given, with every circumstance that may be useful for the purpose of Tracing and Recovering it.

MURDER, AND MALICIOUSLY SHOOTING OR STABBING.

ARSON AND WILFUL BURNING.

ROBBERY FROM THE PERSON.

HOUSE-BREAKING.

HORSE AND CATTLE STEALING.

POLICE GAZETTE
No. 447
April 28, 1832
(352 x 270mm)
'Published by Authority': No sensation. Just reports of recent happenings on the other side of the law.

of the man "walking under water" who amused the inhabitants of Greenwich in his diving suit, the whole paper was occupied with crime.

Bell's Life in London and Sporting Chronicle also concentrated on the seamier side of life. The issue of 16 March 1828 gave prominence to a robbery at Greenock by thieves "of the London school". Headings, hardly headlines, drew attention to "Mysterious Murder at Leighton Buzzard", "Atrocious Burglary", "Seduction Case at Lincoln Assizes", "Incest at Reading", "Execution of Five Men in Front of Newgate". Robert Saunders was indicted for "burglariously breaking and entering". The aggrieved party who had been broken into and entered upon went to the shutters and "the first circumstance that presented itself was a ruffian with a white frock, a

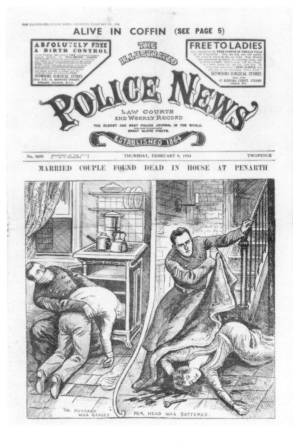

POLICE NEWS
No. 3650
February 8, 1934
(462 x 304mm)
An astonishing survival into the
1930s. Certainly not published
by authority, and with plenty of
sensation.

black face and an iron bar, threatening my life if I
made any resistance". Help was summoned with
the aid of a watchman's rattle and the offender
apprehended.

Public Executions were reported in detail:

> Johnson was next brought under the beam
> on the back of a man, in which position he
> continued till the rope was tied round his
> neck . . . he was supported by three men
> until the drop fell . . . the whole of the
> dreadful preparations being completed, the
> unhappy men were left with their spiritual

NEWS OF THE WORLD
No. 3484
July 31, 1910
(577 x 455mm)
Sunday evening 'Special'
reporting the arrest of 'Dr'
Crippen.

consolers. Johnson and the Younger Melford appeared to suffer much, the others died apparently without a struggle.

Such crime reports can be found in all the popular papers of the 1820s and 1830s. Sensational murders were also turned into the subjects of popular songs, plays and books, particularly the Burke and Hare Murders 1827, and The Murder in the Red Barn, where William Corder killed Maria Marten 1828, but none more so than the Jack the Ripper Murders sixty years later in 1888. The gruesome nature of the crimes combined with the Victorian fascination with East London low-life made the Ripper murders perhaps *the* news story of the century — as well as providing a mass of theorising "Ripperologists". Sales of

129

COWARDLY ATTACK ON THE QUEEN.

We regret exceedingly being called on to announce that an idle miscreant raised his hand against the person of the Sovereign on Saturday evening as her Majesty was returning from an afternoon drive through the Parks. Happily there is not the slightest ground for supposing that the attempt was anything more serious than an endeavour on the part of the wretched man to gain a miserable notoriety. The villain was seized by one of the park-keepers the instant after his hand was raised, and the pistol which he had just discharged having been taken from him, he was dragged off to the police station amidst the execrations of the crowd, who, but for the activity of the police officers and others, would have executed Lynch law upon the miscreant.

The particulars, as far as we have been able to glean, are as follow :—

Her Majesty, after returning from the Drawing Room, left Buckingham Palace shortly before five o'clock in an open carriage and four to take a drive through the Parks. Her Majesty was accompanied in the carriage by their Royal Highnesses Prince Alfred and the Princesses Alice and Helena, and attended by the Hon. Miss Macdonald. His Royal Highness Prince Albert, attended by his equerry, accompanied her Majesty on horseback, and General Wemyss was the Equerry in attendance upon the Queen.

After accompanying her Majesty round the Regent's Park, his Royal Highness Prince Albert took leave of the Queen, and, attended by his Equerry, returned to Buckingham Palace. The Queen followed in a few minutes, and after passing through Hyde Park had gone about 300 yards down Constitution Hill in the direction of the Palace, when a man in the garb of a bricklayer's labourer, who was standing on the green sward within the iron railings, levelled a pistol at the royal carriage, and fired it at the moment the Queen was passing.

Her Majesty heard the report and looked round, but manifested no symptoms of alarm. The royal carriage passed on, almost without the postillions being aware of the occurrence; but General Wemyss instantly pulled up and rode towards the spot whence the report came. Before he could reach the rails the miscreant was in safe custody, having been seized. first by a park-keeper named George Maulden (formerly in the establishment of Lord Palmerston), and subsequently by a police-constable, to neither of whom did he make the slightest resistance. The fellow was taken by the police to Buckingham gate, where a hackney-cab was procured, and was then conveyed to the police-station in Gardiner's-lane, King-street, Westminster, whither he was followed by General Wemyss, the Park-keeper (George Maulden), and other persons who witnessed the transaction which gave rise to his apprehension.

MORNING POST
May 21st, 1849
An assassination attempt on the life of Queen Victoria by 'an idle miscreant'.

London papers rocketed: the *Star* topped 300,000 sales on one night. Londoners scanned all they could lay their hands on to discover the latest reports, as much to be assured for their own safety as out of salacious interest in the grisly mutilations by the undiscovered murderer. The *Illustrated Police News and Law Courts Gazette*, was, despite its official-sounding name, one of the most sensational of the crime journals, adorned with a front page completely filled with "horrible murder" woodcuts, "scenes, views, sketches by artists engaged expressly". The crude, anonymous faces of perpetrators and victims which embellished the pages of the *Police News* would have been at home on the printing blocks that were brought out for use time and time again to provide an "accurate representation" of the prisoner about to be led to the scaffold in the murder and execution broadsides of a century earlier. In recent times, "identi-kit" pictures of suspects seem almost to ape this ancient crudity; Peter Sutcliffe, the so-called "Yorkshire Ripper", who murdered and mutilated 13 women was caught not by recognition but by chance. As in the case of his earlier namesake, it was the newspapers that christened the killer and fanned the fear, and sold extra copies as a result.

The more unusual the murder the bigger the headlines: The Crippen Case 1910, The Brides in the Bath murders 1915, the Heath Case 1946, the Christie-Evans Case which erupted in 1953, and the St Valentine's Day Massacre in Chicago 1930 have been amongst the biggest news stories of all time. Not only murders; all crimes are grist to the newspaper mill; robberies, political and social scandals, kidnappings and plots, corruption, treason, trials; and from the other side of the fence, how the police force operates, and the methods used.

Overleaf:
NEW YORK HERALD
No. 10459
April 15, 1865
(596 x 420mm)
Assassination of the President 1865: Abraham Lincoln shot in his box at Ford's theatre.

THE DAILY TELEGRAPH
No. 33776
November 23, 1963
(590 x 440mm)

THE DALLAS MORNING NEWS
No. 115/54
November 23, 1963
(580 x 412mm)
Assassination of the President 1963: Front pages from London and Dallas.

131

THE NEW YORK HERALD.

WHOLE NO. 10459.　　　　NEW YORK, SATURDAY, APRIL 15, 1865.　　　　PRICE, FOUR CENTS.

IMPORTANT.

ASSASSINATION
OF
PRESIDENT LINCOLN.

The President Shot at the Theatre Last Evening.

SECRETARY SEWARD
DAGGERED IN HIS BED
BUT
NOT MORTALLY WOUNDED.

Clarence and Frederick Seward Badly Hurt.

ESCAPE OF THE ASSASSINS.

Intense Excitement in Washington.

SCENE AT THE DEATHBED OF MR. LINCOLN.

J. Wilkes Booth, the Actor, the Alleged Assassin of the President, &c., &c., &c.

THE OFFICIAL DISPATCH.

THE REBELS.

JEFF. DAVIS AT DANVILLE.

His Latest Appeal to his Deluded Followers.

He Thinks the Fall of Richmond a Blessing in Disguise as it Leaves the Rebel Armies Free to Move From Point to Point.

HE VAINLY PROMISES TO HOLD VIRGINIA AT ALL HAZARDS.

Lee and His Army Supposed to Be Safe.

BRECKINRIDGE AND THE REST OF DAVIS' CABINET REACH DANVILLE SAFELY.

The Organ of Gov. Vance, of North Carolina, Advises the Submission of the Rebels to President Lincoln's Terms.
&c., &c., &c.

JEFF. DAVIS' LAST PROCLAMATION.

EXTRA.
8:10 A. M.

New York, Saturday, April 15, 1865.

DEATH
OF
THE PRESIDENT.

Further Details of the Great Crime.

ADDITIONAL DISPATCHES FROM THE SECRETARY OF WAR.

What is Known of the Assassins.

THE OFFICIAL DISPATCHES.

THE PRESIDENT DEAD.

IMPORTANT FROM SOUTH AMERICA.

Surrender of Montevideo to Gen. Flores — Brazil in Possession of the City, &c.

New Orleans Markets.

600
GEORGE COHEN'S
for PLANT and
MACHINERY
Tel. Sittingbourn Bank 2070

The Daily Telegraph
and Morning Post

No. 33756. LONDON, SATURDAY, NOVEMBER 23, 1963.   Printed in LONDON and MANCHESTER. Price 4d.

DRUMMOND'S
SUITINGS
from quality
of the only consideration

PRESIDENT KENNEDY IS ASSASSINATED

Shot in the head in open car on
Texas festival drive

MRS. KENNEDY COMFORTS HER
WOUNDED HUSBAND

FORMER DEFECTOR TO
RUSSIA ARRESTED

LYNDON JOHNSON SWORN IN
AS NEW PRESIDENT

From STEPHEN BARBER
Daily Telegraph Special Correspondent

DALLAS, Texas, Friday

JOHN FITZGERALD KENNEDY, 46, the 34th President of the United
States, died this afternoon within half-an-hour of being shot in the head
as he drove through Dallas in an open car. He was on his way to make a
speech at a political festival.

The shooting happened at the President's car drove through cheering
crowds. Shots rang out and he slumped down in his seat, hit in the head.

Mrs. Jacqueline Kennedy, who was also in the car, jumped up and cried:
"Oh, no." She cradled her husband in her arms as the car sped to nearby
Parkland Hospital. Police motor-cyclists with sirens blaring cleared a path
through the crowds, and the traffic.

At the hospital President Kennedy was given an immediate blood
transfusion and a Roman Catholic priest was called to his bedside to
administer the last rites. The President died 25 minutes after being shot.

VICE-PRESIDENT ESCAPES INJURY

Vice-President Lyndon Johnson, 55, who was sworn in later as the new

Mrs. Kennedy bending over her husband in the back of the open car after
he had been shot while they were driving through Dallas, Texas. Other
pictures: P9 11, 13, 15 & Back page. The President's life in pictures: P10

JOHNSON TAKES OATH
IN AIRCRAFT

FROM OUR OWN CORRESPONDENT
WASHINGTON, Friday

M

Johnson Takes
Nation - Helm,
Pages 4 and 5

The Dallas Morning News

John F. Kennedy
Life History,
Pages 16 and 17

VOL. 115—NO. 54   DALLAS, TEXAS, SATURDAY, NOVEMBER 23, 1963 — 50 PAGES IN 4 SECTIONS   ★★★★   PRICE 5 CENTS

KENNEDY SLAIN
ON DALLAS STREET

★ ★ ★ ★   ★ ★ ★ ★   ★ ★ ★   ★ ★ ★ ★   ★ ★ ★ ★

JOHNSON BECOMES PRESIDENT

**Receives
Oath on
Aircraft**

By ROBERT E. BASKIN
Washington Bureau of The News

In a solemn and sor-
rowful hour with a na-
tion mourning the dead
President, Lyndon B.
Johnson Friday took the
oath of office as the 36th
chief executive of the
United States.

Following nation, the
oath taking took place
quickly only an hour

**Pro-Communist
Charged With Act**

A sniper shot and killed President John F.
Kennedy on the streets of Dallas Friday. A 24-
year-old pro-Communist who once tried to defect
to Russia was charged with the murder shortly
before midnight.

Kennedy was shot about 12:30 p.m. Friday
at the foot of Elm Street as the Presidential car
neared the approach to the Triple Underpass.
The President died in a sixth-floor surgery room
at Parkland Hospital about 1 p.m., though doctors
said there was no chance for him to live when
he reached the hospital.

Within two hours, Vice-President Lyndon
Johnson was sworn in as the nation's 36th Presi-

DAILY

EXPRESS

Thursday April 30 1981 ● 12p ● Weather : Mainly dry   **THE VOICE OF BRITAIN**

The full court story—See Pages 2, 3, 4, 5 and Jean Rook on the Centre Pages

The Ripper

Peter Sutcliffe goes by prison van to the Old Bailey yesterday where he admitted killing 13 women   Picture by John Rogers

TV Guide Pages 24, 25 • Weather Page 4 • William Hickey Page 13 • Pop Page 26 • Startime Page 31 • Letters Page 32 • Finance Pages 36, 37 • Sport starts Page 39

THE SUBJECT IN QUESTION

Newspapers reflect society, even if the mirror is occasionally a little cracked, and in the same way reflect the interests of anyone who has ever been interested in collecting anything. Subjects are as diverse as the number of entries in an encyclo-paedia.

For those who read their papers backwards, sport comes first. Football got under way in a fairly organised manner over a hundred years ago. The *Observer* of 15 February 1874 reported a game between London and Nottingham played at the Oval:

> The ball was set going soon after 3 o'clock. Nottingham won the toss . . . compelling their opponents to kick off from the goal near the gasometers'

Nottingham played well but were unable to stem the tide against them, London winning 4-0. *Bell's Life in London* for 9 November 1878 reported a match "by Electric Light". Wanderers played Clapham Rovers, again at the Oval, where

> it was endeavoured to throw the light wherever the ball was propelled. This proved to be a great mistake for the rays more often caused the player to lose sight of the ball than to keep possession of it.

More illuminating were the reports of the first Wembley Cup Final between Bolton and West Ham in 1923, or the World Cup Final between England and West Germany in 1966, but to show that nothing is new, the attempts in 1983 by the Chairman of Oxford United Football Club to take over Reading seem to echo from this report of May 1910:

> Considerable surprise was occasioned in the football world on Friday last when it became known that Mr H. G. Norris, of the Fulham Football Club, had informally discussed with the Management Committee of the

Opposite:
DAILY EXPRESS
No. 25132
April 30, 1981
(385 x 298mm)
The dramatic front page at the time of Peter Sutcliffe's trial.

135

Football League a proposal that the Woolwich Arsenal Club and the Fulham Club should be amalgamated and removed to the Fulham ground. It was generally recognised that this proposal would meet with very considerable opposition from all sections of football people . . .

Clearly the proposals met a similar fate to those mooted in 1983.

With match results and league tables being given increasing prominence in newspapers from the 1920s onwards, there is obviously much to interest a present day football fan with an eye for the great footballing events, and players, of the past.

And sport often makes the front page. "AT LAST — THE 4-MINUTE MILE" headlined the *Daily Express* on Friday 7 May 1954.

> The dream of world athletes through the years was achieved yesterday by an Englishman — 25-year-old Roger Bannister, who became the first man on earth to run a mile in under four minutes. His feat at Oxford last evening — against a 20-mile-an-hour cross-wind — was equal in dramatic achievement to the crashing of the sound barrier in the air. Bannister's time, officially recorded, was 3 MINS. 59.4 SECS.

On 27 May 1909, the *Daily Graphic* gave over its front page to the "CROWN DERBY" and photographs of "His Majesty's Minoru receiving a great ovation on entering the weighing-in enclosure after winning the Derby, the first in history won by a sovereign, at Epsom yesterday." In the same issue, Rhodes of Yorkshire was named as one of England's Test Match team to play Australia at cricket; in August 1926, Rhodes ("Cricket's Peter Pan") was still making the front page as England trounced Australia at the Oval to bring back the Ashes after fourteen years. The *Daily Sketch* headline read: "CROWD'S WILD RUSH AFTER TEST MATCH VICTORY".

Above:

THE DAILY GRAPHIC, *April 27, 1901 (395 x 295mm)*
 Cup Final 1901: Artist's impression of the 2-2 draw between Tottenham Hotspur and Sheffield United before 120,000 spectators.

Overleaf:

THE DAILY GRAPHIC, *May 27, 1909 (410 x 290mm)*
 The England cricket team for the First Test against Australia at Edgbaston including Hobbs, Fry and Rhodes. Page 4 of the issue which reported Minoru's win for the King in the Derby.

ENGLAND.

1. W. BRYARLEY (LANCASHIRE).   2. G. L. JESSOP (GLOUCESTERSHIRE).   3. A. O. JONES (NOTTS).   4. RELF (A. E.) (SUSSEX).   5. THOMPSON (NORTHANTS).   6. LILLEY (WARWICKSHIRE).   7. A. C. MACLAREN (LANCASHIRE) (CAPTAIN).   8. HOBBS (SURREY.   9. TYLDESLEY (LANCASHIRE).   10. BLYTHE (KENT).   11. C. B. FRY (HAMPSHIRE).   12. HIRST (YORKSHIRE).   13. HAYWARD (SURREY).   14. RHODES (YORKSHIRE).

THE CRICKETERS FROM WHOM TO-DAY'S ELEVEN WILL BE SELECTED TO REPRESENT ENGLAND IN THE FIRST TEST MATCH AGAINST AUSTRALIA TO BE PLAYED ON THE EDGBASTON GROUND, BIRMINGHAM.

(Photographed by Hawkins, Brighton.)

706

138

THE RACING CALENDAR, No. XV, June 12, 1850 (518 x 345mm)

DAILY EXPRESS, No. 16805, May 7, 1954 (600 x 420mm)

A year after the Crown Derby, Jack Johnson beat James J. Jeffries "thus retaining the title of Heavy-weight Champion of the World". As the *Mirror* put it on 5 July 1910:

> In the fifteenth round Johnson went for Jeffries savagely. Twice Jeffries, who had never been even brought to his knees in any previous battle, was knocked down with a rain of rights and lefts on the face, and on both occasions eight seconds were counted before he rose. The excited crowd shouted "Stop it! Don't let him knock him out!" But the match went on. Jeffries was hurled to the floor again, this time not to rise. As he hung on the ropes, the fatal ten seconds were counted, and the white man was beaten.

Fifty six years later, Henry Cooper had his last stab at the same title against the then Cassius Clay. The *Sunday Mirror* of 22 May 1966 gave over most of its front page to a blood spattered "Gallant Henry". Clay commented on the flow of blood from Cooper's eye that opened up in the sixth round: "You could hear it come . . . I just did not like hitting him."

The development of flight in the twentieth century is a good example of the way in which newspapers reflect modern history. Because of its immediacy and pictorial appeal, breakthroughs have nearly always made headlines from the Wright Brothers, through Bleriot and the early cross-channel attempts, flying shows before the First World War, trans-Atlantic flights between the wars, airships, the role of the aeroplane in the Second World War, development of jet planes, to modern space exploration.

Another example of technology which has continued to have news value, is the communications business, from telephones, through wireless and television to computers.

Above:
THE DAILY MIRROR
No. 2087, July 5, 1910
(385 x 302mm)

Right: SUNDAY MIRROR
No. 163
May 22, 1966
(374 x 302mm)

141

SOUTH POLE DISASTER.

CAPTAIN SCOTT AND FOUR COMRADES PERISH.

DEATH FROM WANT AND EXPOSURE.

TRAGIC FATE AFTER REACHING THE GOAL.

---

11 MILES TO SAFETY.

PATHETIC VOYAGE OF MRS. SCOTT.

The tragic news reached London yesterday that Captain Scott, the leader of the British Antarctic expedition, and four of his followers perished nearly a year ago while returning to their main base after successfully reaching the South Pole.

No word had been received of the courageous band of explorers since early last year, when the Terra Nova brought the news to New Zealand that Captain Scott and his southern party had left for the final stage in their journey to the Pole. It is the Terra Nova which now brings the news of the disaster.

TWO DAYS FOR RECONSTRUCTION OF CABINET—COMMONS ADJOURN

The Daily Mirror

CERTIFIED CIRCULATION LARGER THAN THAT OF ANY OTHER DAILY PICTURE PAPER

No. 4093   TUESDAY, DECEMBER 5, 1916   One Halfpenny.

ONE OF THE MOST HEROIC RESCUES IN HISTORY: SIR ERNEST SHACKLETON'S 750-MILE VOYAGE IN A SMALL BOAT.

Above:
THE DAILY MIRROR, No. 4093
December 5, 1916 (385 x 300mm)
Shackleton's return after failing to reach the South Pole.

Left:
DAILY EXPRESS
No. 4008, February 11, 1913
The death of Scott — 'after reaching the goal'

Going where no man has gone before makes news. Stanley meeting Livingstone, Hillary and Tensing climbing Everest, Shackleton failing to reach the South Pole or Scott failing to return are the stories which people want to read about, and subsequently become absorbed into the history of exploration.

DAILY EXPRESS, No. 17935, January 22, 1958 (600 x 395mm)
Meeting at the South Pole: 'radioed direct from the Antarctic'.

Above:
DAILY GRAPHIC, No. 9123, March 7, 1919 (400 x 305mm)
Trials for the R33 airship, 'the biggest airship so far constructed' at Selby, Yorkshire.

DAILY EXPRESS, No. 13604, January 7, 1944 (600 x 420mm)
Public announcement of the invention of the jet by Frank Whittle — kept secret since its first flight in 1941.

DAILY EXPRESS, No. 17844, October 5, 1957 (600 x 395mm)
A perceptive headline announcing the launching of the first Sputnik.

Left:
LOS ANGELES SUNDAY TIMES
September 12, 1926
A somewhat premature report, apparently written in good faith.

Below:
DAILY MIRROR, No. 20393
July 21, 1969 (392 x 300mm)

146

The subject in question can also be a person or a place. The great names make news throughout their lives. Churchill's career is a spectacular example: Soldier, Member of Parliament, Minister, newspaper editor (the *British Gazette* during the 1926 General Strike), war leader. A home town can be the place on which a collection is based — local history as reflected in local papers, reports of major events in the town which have made the national press.

These are just a handful of suggestions. The scope is endless. Whatever the interest, newspapers of the day will provide a new perspective on what might otherwise be thought of as the dry dust of history.

DAILY EXPRESS, February 13, 1925
A cartoon based on a popular packet of cigarettes when it was rumoured that Mr Winston Churchill, the Chancellor of the Exchequer, was going to increase the tax on tobacco.

The Daily Mirror

THE MORNING JOURNAL WITH THE SECOND LARGEST NET SALE.

No. 1,522.   Registered at the G. P. O. as a Newspaper.   MONDAY, SEPTEMBER 14, 1908.   One Halfpenny.

MR. WINSTON CHURCHILL MARRIED TO MISS CLEMENTINE HOZIER AT ST. MARGARET'S, WESTMINSTER.

The most popular and interesting wedding of the year took place on Saturday at St. Margaret's, Westminster, when Mr. Winston Churchill, President of the Board of Trade, married Miss Clementine Hozier, daughter of Lady Blanche Hozier and the late Colonel Sir Henry Hozier, in the presence of over a thousand guests, many of them distinguished in politics, science, art, and literature. An enormous crowd assembled in Parliament-square to see the arrival and departure of the bride and bridegroom. (1) Miss Hozier arrives with her brother, Sub-Lieutenant Hozier, R.N. (2) Mr. and Mrs. Churchill leaving the church. (3) Miss Nellie Hozier, chief bridesmaid, with her brother. (4) The other four bridesmaids—(a) Miss Madeleine Whyte, (b) Miss Clare Frewen, (c) the Hon. Venetia Stanley, (d) Miss Horatia Seymour.

Opposite:
THE DAILY MIRROR
No. 1522
September 14, 1908
(385 x 300mm)
The President of the Board of Trade marries.

Right
EMERGENCY PRESS — TODAY'S PAPER
April 6, 1955
(372 x 264mm)
With Fleet Street on strike, it was left to an Emergency Press *free-sheet to report the news of Churchill's final resignation as Prime Minister.*

EMERGENCY PRESS

TO-DAY'S PAPER

WEDNESDAY, 6th APRIL, 1955

FAREWELL, SIR WINSTON

WELCOME, SIR ANTHONY

SIR WINSTON CHURCHILL is no longer Prime Minister. Last night the greatest man of the 20th Century handed in his resignation to the Queen. He is being succeeded by Sir Anthony Eden.

Crowds thronged the streets of Whitehall and sang "For He's A Jolly Good Fellow" as the Grand Old Man left No. 10 Downing Street to lay down the seals of office.

He waved his cigar in a characteristic gesture as he left the Palace after seeing the Queen.

Then his historic drive back through the streets ended yet another chapter in Britain's History.

London and the whole of Britain today salutes the great man who saved Britain during the darkest days of the war.

His great speeches during the black days of Hitler's blitz on London will never be forgotten.

It is these speeches that Londoners deprived of the newspapers which would have done honour to him today, had they been published, will remember and recall with pride and emotion.

Speeches like this:—

"I have nothing to offer but blood, toil, tears and sweat. We have before us an ordeal of the most grievous kind."

And like this:—

"We shall fight in France and we shall fight on the seas and oceans. We shall fight with growing confidence and growing strength in the air ... we shall fight on the beaches, we shall fight on the landing grounds, we shall fight in the fields and in the streets, we shall fight in the hills, we shall never surrender."

It was these speeches that inspired Britain to fight on against the odds.

From War to Peace

He united the country, rich and poor, Tories and Socialists. He created the great War Cabinet from all parties. It was he who guided the country through difficult negotiations with America and then with Russia.

It was he who was at the helm when peace in Europe was finally declared on May 8, 1945, that night when the crowds gathered in Whitehall—as they did last night—to sing "For He's A Jolly Good Fellow."

Sir Winston was born in 1874. He was educated at Harrow. In 1908 he married Miss Clementine Ogilvy Hozier. She was 23.

She has been at his side during four reigns. They have four children—Randolph, Diana, Sarah and Mary.

He served in the South African War 1899–1900 and was taken prisoner but escaped.

In the 1914–1918 war he served as a lieutenant-colonel in the Royal Scots Fusiliers.

After Sir Winston resigned, an announcement from Buckingham Palace said: "He rendered his resignation, which Her Majesty was most graciously pleased to accept."

Earlier, Sir Winston presided over a full meeting of the Cabinet. A big crowd waited outside after his audience with the Queen. He waved his hand in a V-sign and the crowd sang "For He's A Jolly Good Fellow."

In Good Cheer

Sir Winston laid down the burden of office with apparent good cheer. But though he is no longer the Prime Minister of Great Britain, he is still a member of the House of Commons as M.P. for Woodford, Essex.

Sir Winston does not immediately cease office: he will carry on formally until Sir Anthony Eden is installed.

At No. 10 Downing Street, on his return from the Palace, cheer after cheer went up from the crowd. He lifted his top hat in salute and waved his cigar. The crowd, who had been waiting for hours, were swept with emotion.

His audience with the Queen lasted only 12 minutes. Within those minutes one of the greatest political figures in history had left the scene, still young at 80.

Sir Winston, speaking at a dinner at No. 10 the previous night, when the Queen and the Duke of Edinburgh were present, said he wanted to express deeply his lively sense of gratitude to the Royal Family, and referred to the Queen as a "young, gleaming champion."

The Queen in reply proposed Sir Winston's health.

Billy Graham and peace

DOCTOR BILLY GRAHAM, the Evangelist, told 7,000 at Redford Barracks, Edinburgh: "We are living in a period of world history that is the most critical and crucial to the human race. This is a solemn hour, and our intellectual and military leaders and our diplomats are all searching for the answer.

"In the last 2,000 years there had been only 257 years of peace. We are looking for peace; we want peace. How are we going to find it?"

He had heard that H-bombs were big enough to form a deterrent to war, but he asked: "How many of us would say that Hitler in his last days would have hesitated to push the button and make the whole world a funeral pyre if he had it within his power?"

STOP PRESS

Cheaper Coal again this Summer

IN reply to questions in the House of Commons about the supply and distribution of coal, Mr. Joynson-Hicks, Parliamentary Secretary, Ministry of Fuel and Power, announced that summer prices were again to be introduced this year to enable house-holders to stock-up for the winter.

He said that for the twelve months ending February 28, 1955, 4,235,000 tons of coal were imported, of which 935,000 tons were from Canada and 3,300,000 tons from other sources.

In the twelve months to March 31, 30,500,000 tons of coal were sold to house-holders, and it was estimated that about 32,500,000 tons might be required if household coal were derestricted.

See inside for Sport

WEST-END FILMS

CARLTON, Haymarket
"A Man Called Peter," Richard Todd, Jean Peters. CinemaScope. Colour by De Luxe (U).

EMPIRE, Leicester Square
"Deep In My Heart," 20 stars, 22 song hits. Print by Technicolor (U).

GAUMONT, Haymarket
"Foxfire," Jane Russell, Jeff Chandler, Dan Duryea. Colour by Technicolor (A).
"A Life In The Balance," Ricardo Montalban, Anne Bancroft (A).

LEICESTER SQ. Theatre
"The Night My Number Came Up," Michael Redgrave, Sheila Sim, Alexander Knox, Denholm Elliott (U).
"Attenborough and [illegible] Devils on the Barrier Reef." Colour by Eastman Colour (U).

LONDON PAVILION
"Lucretia Borgia," Martine Carol, Pedro Armendariz. Colour by Technicolor (A).

ODEON, Leicester Square
"Above Us the Waves," John Mills, John Gregson, Donald Sinden (U).

ODEON, Marble Arch
"White Feather," Robert Wagner, John Lund, Debra Paget. CinemaScope. Colour by Technicolor (U).

PLAZA, Piccadilly Circus
"The Country Girl," Bing Crosby, Grace Kelly, William Holden (A).

RIALTO, Coventry Street
"Carmen Jones," Dorothy Dandridge, Harry Belafonte. CinemaScope. Colour by De Luxe (A).

RITZ, Leicester Square
"Prisoner of War," Ronald Reagan, Dewey Martin, Steve Forrest (X).

WARNER, Leicester Square
"A Star is Born," Judy Garland, James Mason. CinemaScope. Colour by Technicolor (A).

"ALL YOUR MAP PROBLEMS SOLVED"
GEOGRAPHERS' MAP CO., LTD.
24 GRAYS' INN ROAD, HOLBORN, LONDON, W.C.1
Telephones:– General Offices CHAncery 3824/5 — Showrooms CHAncery 9246

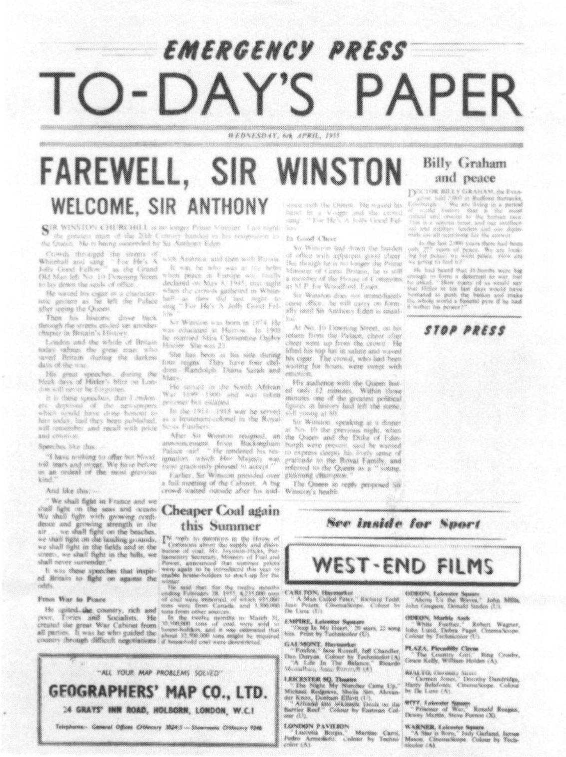

DAILY MAIL, No. 15358, July 27, 1945 (600 x 420mm)
NEWS CHRONICLE, No. 31137, March 1946 (600 x 424mm)
SUNDAY TELEGRAPH, No. 209, January 31, 1965 (600 x 432mm)

III. PRINTING HISTORY — DEVELOPMENT OF DESIGN AND ILLUSTRATION

The Empire Crusader of Beaverbrook Newspapers from the DAILY EXPRESS masthead, January 25, 1936 (11,138).

In between the first and final issues (assuming that the newspaper has kept going for more than a few years), there will be major changes in layout, in the number of columns, use of illustrations, headlines, masthead [or title], typography [typefaces and sizes of type used], sort of illustrations, drawings, photographs, the style in which the paper is written and the material it contains.

These changes are clearly more common in the twentieth century. The *Daily Herald*, for example, went through thirteen major front-page design and masthead changes between 1940 and its death in 1964. On the other hand *The Times* had a very similar front page appearance (to the layman) in the 1960s as it did in the 1820s — completely covered with classified advertisements until, on 3 May 1966, news finally reached the front page. Of course, *The Times* had gone through various design changes before that, notably Stanley Morison's typographical changes of 1932. The subtleties of newspaper design, which become more fascinating the more you know about them, are excellently described in the late Allen Hutt's *The Changing Newspaper* published in 1973 and indispensable to a collector interested in this aspect of the press.

Illustration has a fundamental influence on page layout. Woodcuts — drawings cut in printing blocks — were used in early newspamphlets, but these were often used time and again for different purposes. A full-rigged ship and a pair of dolphins would do quite well to represent a naval battle. One of the first uses of a "topical" illustration, a "true portraiture of the poysined knife both in length and breadth" in a newspamphlet describing an attempted assassination of the Duke of Buckingham. In the 1640s the Diurnalls and Mercuries often incorporated standard woodcuts in their headings; *Mercurius Civicus, London's Intelligencer* 1643-1646 was the first newspaper to

THE ILLUSTRATED LONDON NEWS

No. 666.—VOL. XXIV.]   SATURDAY, FEBRUARY 4, 1854.   [WITH TWO SUPPLEMENTS, 1s.

THE QUEEN'S SPEECH.

It may be doubted whether the civilised world ever offers so grand a spectacle as the opening of the British Parliament by Queen Victoria in person. The muster and parade of armies may be more brilliant, and, in many respects, more attractive to the taste of Continental Sovereigns and their people; but the annual assemblage of the Legislature of this free country is an event that appeals to higher faculties and emotions. It rises far above such merely physical displays as these. Despotic Monarchs are obliged to surround themselves with troops of armed men, and to mimic, even in peaceful ceremonials, the rude scenic effects of warfare, whenever on any great occasions they desire to make their royalty appreciated by a show-loving and hero-worshipping multitude. The scene when her Majesty, surrounded by her Court and by the Great Ministers of State takes her seat upon the throne in the House of Lords, is one of great beauty and magnificence in itself, but it has a moral significance and importance which vastly enhance its splendour, and make military parade of the most imposing kind appear vulgar and poor in comparison. It not only pleases the eye and fills the imagination, but it satisfies the judgment of the spectator. It may be said to do even more than this; for, rightly considered, it should increase his proper self-esteem and elevate in his own estimation the dignity of his citizenship. Those who witness a sight so brilliant, and even the countless thousands who read of it in the public journals, cannot but reflect, when her Majesty addresses the assemblage before her, that the speaker is the Sovereign of the greatest, and one of the most ancient empires in the world; whose fleets are in every sea, and whose power and commerce pervade the earth; that the individuals to whom her words are more immediately directed are a rich, intelligent, and popular aristocracy—who, by themselves, or their ancestors, have always proved themselves the friends of the liberty of the people; and the members of the House of Com-

ADMIRAL SLADE (MUCHAVER PACHA), OTTOMAN NAVY.

(SEE NEXT PAGE.)

mons—the most illustrious legislative body that ever existed in any country. They cannot but remember that its few and well-considered sentences which fall from the Royal lips are intended not only for the ears of those who are privileged to listen, but for the great English people in every part of the world—and, next to them, for the consideration and criticism of all civilised nations that can by any possibility be involved in our politics or interested in our progress.

The circumstances of Europe gave to the usual State ceremonial of Tuesday last an importance which no similar anniversary has had at any period within the recollection of the present generation. The great question of peace or war did not, it is true, depend for its solution upon the words which the responsible Ministers of Queen Victoria advised their Sovereign to utter; but the anxiety of the nation was excited in the highest degree to know whether those words would assert the dignity of the British Empire; and the determination of its Government to do its best to maintain the equilibrium of Europe, by peaceful means, as long as peaceful means were both honourable and possible; and by warlike means whenever it became evident that the public disturber was not to be influenced by any other. The Speech has not belied expectation. The Emperor of Russia—who never appears to have believed that Great Britain and France were in earnest until their squadrons were in the Euxine—will understand, and, it is to be hoped, appreciate it. The immediate increase both of our military and naval armaments which the Speech, in its opening paragraph, so significantly announces, if it do not help the Czar to a pacific conclusion, will show the wavering Courts and Cabinets of Europe which side they had better take, if they wish to preserve themselves intact amid the impending crash, which is certain to follow on every point against which the united forces of Great Britain and France shall be directed. The result of the war—if war is to come—will be loss of power, of prestige, and of position to Russia; but to Austria, if she prefer a Russian alliance in a wrongful cause to a British

ADMIRAL SLADE'S (MUCHAVER PACHA'S) FLAG-SHIP "NUSRETIEH," "VICTORIOUS."—(SEE NEXT PAGE.)

Opposite:
THE ILLUSTRATED
LONDON NEWS
No. 666
February 4, 1854
(405 x 280mm)
The most successful illustrated
weekly newspaper of the
nineteenth century. This issue
reports the Opening of
Parliament just before the
declaration of hostilities
between Britain and Russia in
the Crimea.

The Times

be regularly illustrated with a variety of wood-cuts. The first substantial illustration in any English-language newspaper was that of a volcano in the *Weekly Newes* of December 1638.

Little use of illustration was made in the eighteenth century except for the occasional political cartoon or layout of a battle plan. In April 1806, an issue of *The Times* carried a plan of the house in which a murder had taken place and this was regarded as quite an innovation. The steel-engraved plate, introduced in the 1820s and 1830s for book illustration, was not taken up by newspapers until much later. Even the cruder woodcuts which had been available for use since the beginnings of newspaper history were seldom employed. The *Illustrated London News*, founded in 1842, was the first weekly newspaper to carry topical engravings. Its advantages were that it was weekly and could therefore spend more time on preparing illustrations, and also it was printed on better quality paper. The first issue contained a fine engraved view of the conflagration of the city of Hamburg. It was a popular journal, and issues were as a matter of course bound into half-yearly volumes, which are readily available for most years. These are often "broken" by booksellers into individual issues, or the woodcut illustrations extracted and mounted.

The big problem, even for a weekly newspaper, was the simple fact that while news could be quickly transferred into type, it took at least another week for drawings of a scene to be transferred into an engraving. For instance, the issue of the *Illustrated London News* reporting the fall of the Tay Bridge came out in the last week of 1879, while the pictures appeared the week after.

The first issue of the *Illustrated London News* coincided with an early form of photography, the Daguerreotype. Experimental photographs were taken of the Hamburg fire at the same time as *Illustrated London News* artist-correspondent was drawing the scene, but it was almost another forty years before photographs were employed by newspapers. The half-tone printing process necessary to reproduce them was perfected in America in 1880 and the first newspaper photograph appeared in the *New York Daily Graphic* in the same year. The cheap illustrated papers in Britain, like the *Police Gazette*, began to use zinc phototype blocks for reproducing artists' sketches in the 1880s. The slowness with which the daily press took up the idea of illustration, let alone photographs, is clearly demonstrated by the London *Graphic*, Britain's first illustrated daily, which employed only engraved line blocks of drawings when it appeared for the first time in 1890. By 1892, the *Illustrated London News* was using photographs regularly, but it was not until the *Daily Illustrated Mirror* (it soon dropped the *Illustrated* in the title) of 7 January 1904 the first daily paper to be exclusively illustrated with photographs on the front and back and centre-spread, that "photo-journalism" really began.

In the ten years up to the First World War, newspaper photography developed from portraits and views into real news-pictures; by the 1920s, half-tones were being regularly used by all papers. Since then, the techniques have remained very much the same in terms of taking, processing and printing photographs; only the way in which they are used has changed to suit the evolution of style and layout. It has proved impossible to satisfactorily combine colour illustrations in the majority of national newspapers which are still printed on high-speed rotary letter-press machines. Some papers, mainly local, which are now printed by the web-offset process are able to include topical colour illustrations. The nationals have overcome this, and at the same time taken advantage of the dearth of colour-illustrated news magazines, by producing colour-magazines with varying degrees of success. The longest surviving colour magazine is that which accompanies the *Sunday Times*. It first appeared in February 1962.

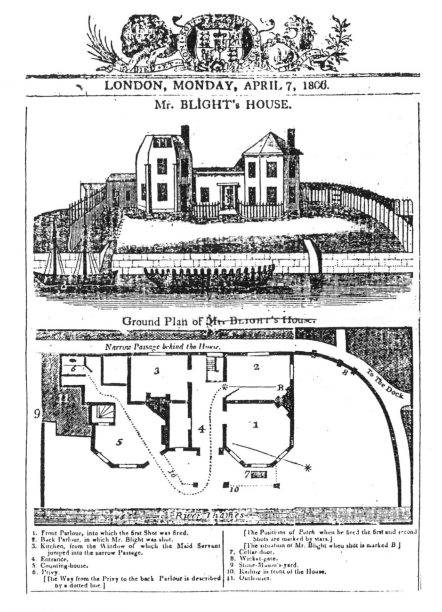

Mr. BLIGHT's HOUSE.

Ground Plan of Mr. Blight's House.

Narrow Passage behind the House.

To The Dock

River Thames

1. Front Parlour, into which the first Shot was fired.
2. Back Parlour, in which Mr. Blight was shot.
3. Kitchen, from the Window of which the Maid Servant jumped into the narrow Passage.
4. Entrance.
5. Counting-house.
6. Privy.
   [The Way from the Privy to the back Parlour is described by a dotted line.]

[The Positions of Patch when he fired the first and second Shots are marked by stars.]
[The situation of Mr. Blight when shot is marked B.]
7. Cellar-door.
8. Wicket-gate.
9. Stone-Mason's-yard.
10. Railing in front of the House.
11. Outhouses.

THE TIMES, April 7, 1806
Early use of a front page woodcut illustrating the murder scene. Trial of Isaac Patch for the murder of Isaac Blight. Verdict: Guilty.

155

Left:
THE PENNY
ILLUSTRATED PAPER
No. 1476
September 14, 1889
(400 x 296mm)
Popular illustrated journal of
the 1880s; an issue which
reported the 'ninth horrible
murder in Whitechapple' by
Jack the Ripper.

Right:
THE GRAPHIC
1901
Woodcut blocks were still being
widely used for illustrations
after 1900, though slowly giving
way to the half-tone reproduc-
tion of an artist's impression or
an actual photograph (see over-
page).

Opposite:
THE GRAPHIC
1901
Artistic recreation still had to
do for the dramatic;
photographs could only be used
for the more static.

A DETACHMENT OF THE 1st MOUNTED INFANTRY RECONNOITRING IN AN ARMOURED TRAIN

OPERATIONS IN THE ORANGE RIVER COLONY: GOING TO THE RESCUE OF A TRAIN HELD UP BY THE BOERS

From a Photograph by a Private Officer

The Royal party arrived at the jetty by the railway leading to the dockyard shown in the foreground. The South Railway Jetty has seen thousands of troops and bluejackets leave for South Africa lately, and the scene on Saturday when the *Ophir* sailed was a striking contrast to the departure of troopships. Our photograph is by Stephen Cribb, Southsea.

H.M.S. "OPHIR" LYING AT THE SOUTH RAILWAY JETTY, PORTSMOUTH, BEFORE HER DEPARTURE

THE DUKE AND DUCHESS OF CORNWALL'S COLONIAL TOUR

157

Examples of the numerous changes in the style and typefaces employed by the DAILY HERALD between 1941 and 1962.

ADVERTISING HISTORY — INFORMATION AND PERSUASION

Newspaper advertisements are to newspaper news what autobiography is to the narrative of a man's life told by another. The paragraphs tell us *about* men's sayings and doings; the advertisements *are* their sayings and doings . . . There is a dramatic interest about the advertising columns which belongs to no other department of a newspaper. They tell us what men are busy about, how they feel, what they think, what they want . . . we have the whole busy ant-hill of city life exposed to view . . .

Charles Knight's introduction to the subject in his *London Magazine* of the 1840s ignores perhaps the basic motive of advertising — making money — on the part of both the newspaper proprietors and the advertisers, but in the 1840s the largest advertisements were hardly ever more than a few inches square. In the advertising columns of *The Times*, personal advertisements nestled side-by-side with much more commercial ones. The brother is implored to come home; the gentleman who has left a blue coat on a cab offers 10s reward for its return; the rhinoceros cane lost in Cider Cellars, Maiden Lane, is Sought after; "a young and protectionless orphan lady" appeals for £200, while at the same time and in the next column the quacks extol the virtues of their dubious products.

The roots of the advertisement were indeed non-commercial. The word itself means "information", offered publicly. The very first advertisement is not generally agreed upon, but two contenders are in the running for the title. On 2 April 1647 in *Perfect Occurrences of Every Day's Journall in Parliament*, mention is made of "a book applauded by the clergy of England called *The Divine Right of Church Government* collected by sundry eminent Ministers of the City of London"; and in the *Impartial Intelligencer* 1-7 March 1648 appeared a notice from a gentleman at Candish, Suffolk, offering a reward for two horses that had been stolen.

159

The Times.

Nº. 21,532.   LONDON, TUESDAY, SEPTEMBER 18, 1852.   PRICE 5d.

THE
PALL MALL GAZETTE
A Morning Newspaper and Review.

No. 1.—Vol. I.   SATURDAY, JANUARY 1, 1870.   Price 2d.; Stamped, 3d.

The Standard.

No. 19,116.   LONDON, TUESDAY, OCTOBER 20, 1885.   ONE PENNY.

Opposite:
THE TIMES
No. 21532
September 13, 1853
(630 x 464mm)

THE PALL MALL
GAZETTE
No. 1
January 1, 1870
(580 x 412mm)
Front pages quite solid with
advertisements, though the Pall
Mall Gazette *shows some signs*
of improvement.

THE STANDARD
No. 19116
October 20, 1885
(645 x 495mm)

What started as an adjunct to the main business of the newspaper, supplying news and information, changed, particularly as a result of the Industrial Revolution, to become a vital part of the newspaper industry. In this century, at least up to the beginning of the 1970s, advertising has been the main reason why the selling price of most papers stayed at or below the price level of 1900 in relative terms. In the nineteenth century, combined with the removal of punitive taxes and increasing circulations, advertising enabled the cover price to fall from about 10d in 1800 to ¼d. in 1900.

For the reader today, the advertisements of the past are often the gems in otherwise uninteresting newspapers. Many have a simplicity and honesty, or a downright dishonesty, which are a refreshing change from the carefully chosen words of present day advertisers anxious not to infringe consumer-protection legislation, not actually saying, but implying, merit. The editor of the *Collection for the Improvement of Husbandry and Trade* 1682-1703 (an early trade paper) told his readers in one issue:

> I have met with a curious gardener, that will furnish anybody that sends to me for fruit-trees and floreal shrubs and garden seeds. I have made him promise, with all solemnnity, that whatever he sends me shall be purely good and I verily believe he may be depended on.

This advertiser in the *Tatler* No. 70, 1710, made rather more exaggerated claims:

> An incomparable Beautifying Cream for the Face, Neck and Hands, takes away all freckles, Spots, Pimples, Wrinkles, Roughness, Scurf, Morphew, Yellowness, Sunburning, renders the Skin admirably Clear,

161

GAS ECONOMY.—Saving, Safety, Convenience.—
CARNABY'S PATENT APPARATUS for turning on and
off and regulating the supply from any part of the premises.—
CARNABY and CO., 13, Broad-street, Bloomsbury, W.C.

DOUGHTY'S VOICE LOZENGES.
For the Voice in Health.
For the Voice in Health.
For the Voice in Health.

DOUGHTY'S VOICE LOZENGES.
For Singers.
For Singers.
For Singers.

DOUGHTY'S VOICE LOZENGES.
The Fragrant Confection.
The Fragrant Confection.
The Fragrant Confection.

DOUGHTY'S VOICE LOZENGES.
Ask for Doughty's.
Ask for Doughty's.
Ask for Doughty's.

DOUGHTY'S VOICE LOZENGES.
For Speakers.
For Speakers.
For Speakers.

DOUGHTY'S VOICE LOZENGES.
One Shilling. Of Chemists.
One Shilling. Of Chemists.
One Shilling. Of Chemists.

APOLLINARIS.
HIGHEST AWARD,
London, 1884.

"Apollinaris reigns alone
among
Natural Dietetic Table Waters."

HOP BITTERS.
Cures Dyspepsia.
Cures Dyspepsia.
Cures Dyspepsia.

HOP BITTERS.
The great appetiser.
The great appetiser.
The great appetiser.

HOP BITTERS.
The best family medicine.
The best family medicine.
The best family medicine.

HOP BITTERS.
Cures Kidney and Liver Complaint
Cures Kidney and Liver Complaint
Cures Kidney and Liver Complaint

HOP BITTERS.
Cures Nervousness and General Debili
Cures Nervousness and General Debili
Cures Nervousness and General Debili

HOP BITTERS.—Sold by all Chemists
Venders. Prepared only by Hop Bitters Cor
Testimonials of most extraordinary cures sent on a
pamphlet describing form and style of genuine Ho

Left:
THE DAILY TELEGRAPH
No. 9520
November 28, 1885
Before display advertisements,
repetition emphasised the
message.

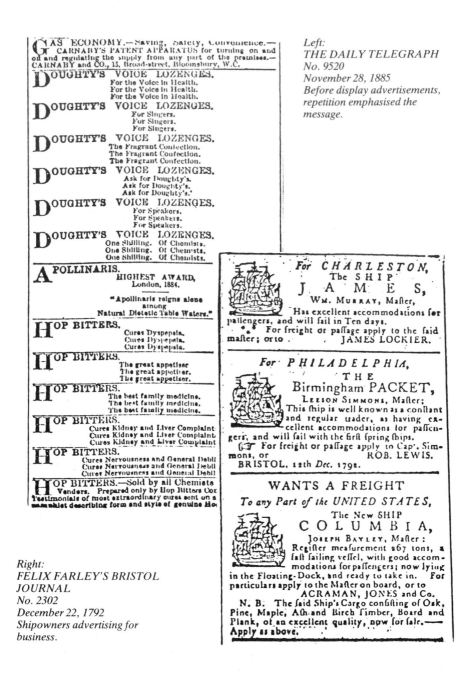

For CHARLESTON,
The SHIP
J A M E S,
WM. MURRAY, Master,
Has excellent accommodations for
passengers, and will sail in Ten days.
For freight or passage apply to the said
master; or to . JAMES LOCKIER.

For PHILADELPHIA,
THE
Birmingham PACKET,
LEESON SIMMONS, Master;
This ship is well known as a constant
and regular trader, as having ex-
cellent accommodations for passen-
gers, and will sail with the first spring ships.
For freight or passage apply to Cap. Sim-
mons, or ROB. LEWIS.
BRISTOL, 12th Dec. 1792.

WANTS A FREIGHT
To any Part of the UNITED STATES,
The New SHIP
C O L U M B I A,
JOSEPH BAYLEY, Master:
Register measurement 267 tons, a
fast sailing vessel, with good accom-
modations for passengers; now lying
in the Floating-Dock, and ready to take in. For
particulars apply to the Master on board, or to
ACRAMAN, JONES and Co.
N. B. The said Ship's Cargo consisting of Oak,
Pine, Maple, Ash and Birch Timber, Board and
Plank, of an excellent quality, now for sale.——
Apply as above.

Right:
FELIX FARLEY'S BRISTOL
JOURNAL
No. 2302
December 22, 1792
Shipowners advertising for
business.

Fair and Beautiful, has an excellent pretty scent; is very safe and harmless, and vastly transcends all other Things; for it truly nourishes the Skin, making it instantly look Plump, Fresh and Smooth and Delicately Fair, though before Wrinkled and Discolour'd, sold only at Mr Lawrence's Toyshop at the Griffin, the corner of the Poultry near Cheapside at 2s 6d a Gally-pot with directions.

The *Daily Advertiser* was the most successful advertising medium in the eighteenth century, but *The Times* became the first large-circulation paper to really take advantage of advertising revenue. The 1820s were a decade of economic expansion and newspaper readership; *The Times* was the leading newspaper and its advertising columns expanded rapidly, almost to an embarrassing extent. Supplements were produced to accommodate excess advertisements on which Stamp Duty had to be paid. Above a certain number of extra advertisement pages, *The Times'* manager told a Select Committee investigating newspaper Stamp Duties in 1851, such supplements would lose money.

With *The Times'* fall from grace as the "National Oracle" during the 1870s and 1880s, the advertising which *The Times* had previously attracted was spread out among its competitors. Some of these were geared to a class of the population which had never before bought a paper, but had money to spend on goods advertised.

"Display" advertising did not become common until the late nineteenth century. The *Daily Telegraph* carried the first "box ad." in the late 1850s, *The Times* following in 1866. By 1900, the *Graphic*, for instance, was filled with well-designed, illustrated advertising. By that date, the advertisements had become the most attractive part of the newspaper, setting trends in layout and design. Some series of advertisements of this

period, such as those for Lifebuoy Soap and Bovril, have become classics; when printed on better quality paper, they make attractive pictures in themselves. Issues containing such attractive advertisements are often inexpensive, and the collector has the advantage of being able to find just what he or she is looking for in a newspaper that otherwise would not be of interest to anyone.

In general, keeping complete newspapers rather than sections or pages is preferable. With an advertising theme, there is perhaps a stronger argument for just retaining relevant pages, particularly where the theme is the historical development of the advertising of a particular commodity such as cars or cigarettes for instance.

Opposite:
DAILY MAIL, September 17, 1917 (588 x 443mm)
War-time but fashion-conscious Britain as reflected in the front-page of the Daily Mail *'the paper that is saving tonnage'. 'Dark Blinds and Curtains to comply with the lighting regulations' from 11¾d per yard; 'No item of dress is more important than the corset, for it is the foundation upon which the whole toilette depends' opines the copywriter for Peter Robinson's, while Derry & Toms' Stuart Bedroom Suite is offered at £12.15.0d.*

Overleaf:
THE DAILY EXPRESS, December 5, 1931 (594 x 425mm)
A page of 'Modern Homes' from 1931; Seven-roomed villas from £888 freehold, '£38 down, Not another farthing'. Prefabricated bungalows from £60, 26/6d a week repayments for houses in Croydon; 'View of open country . . . free from fog'.

V. CURIOSITIES OF THE PRESS

MAN BITES DOG

"Dog bites man" is not news; "Man bites dog" is, and man has bitten dog many times, if newspaper reports over the years are to be believed.

"Man Bites Man" is the title given to a selection of press-cuttings collected by George Ives between the Edwardian period and 1950, published in 1980. Ives, described as "eccentric" and "clipster-extraordinary", clearly had an eye for the bizarre. Whenever he spotted an unlikely story, he cut it out and pasted it into one of his black-and-gold books. Typical is the following from a 1917 newspaper:

> 72 YEARS SPENT IN BED. Extraordinary Love Tragedy Recalled.
> An old lady's death in Scarborough recalls a remarkable tragedy of disappointed love.
> When she was 21 years of age she contracted an engagement which did not meet with the approval of her father, who forbade it. The young lady in her disappointment took to her bed, where she remained until her death, except that on one occasion she rose to leave Cambridge for Scarborough.
> She never suffered from any complaint until the end, when she was ill for only two days. She died at the age of 94, and had therefore been in bed for seventy-two years.

Ives' collection, published by Penguin Books, is a remarkable compilation of the weird and wonderful. He does not include misprints and unintentional *double-entendres* another source of harmless amusement to newspaper readers, both equally collectable.

Newspapers are sometimes tricked into publishing the untrue. The "Parnell Letters" forged by Richard Pigott in 1888 landed *The Times* in court. Almost one hundred years later, the *Sunday Times* fell for what appeared to be a fantastic scoop and turned out to be an obvious forgery — the Hitler Diaries.

On the 23rd January, 1882, *The Times* printed a long report of a speech by Sir William Harcourt, the Home Secretary. It included an obscene expression which greatly offended most of the paper's readers, but apparently delighted others. Urgent telegraph messages called in all unsold copies and by mid-morning they were said to be changing hands at up to 12s 6d each as against a normal price of 5d.

THE TIMES
January 23rd, 1882

you the truth, I do not think that the particular issue of this election is so important as the principles upon which it is being fought. (Hear, hear.) The farmers are beginning to think and act for themselves. They may cast their votes in this instance or that instance, in one way or in another, but when once they begin to take an active and intelligent interest in politics, when they begin to understand the advantage of being represented by one of themselves, or by those who thoroughly understand their interest, then I have very little doubt to which side in politics their influence will ultimately incline. (Cheers.) The tenant-farmers are a very shrewd class of people, and if once they understand that they have the power if they choose to deal with their own affairs, you may depend upon it they will deal with them very sensibly. (Cheers.) I saw in a Tory journal the other day a note of alarm, in which they said, "Why, if a tenant-farmer is elected for the North Riding of Yorkshire the farmers will be a political power who will have be reckoned with." The speaker then said he felt inclined for a bit of fucking. I think that is very likely. (Laughter.) But I think it is rather an extraordinary thing that the Tory party have not found that out before. I had some experience of it in the Ground Game Bill, which my friend, Sir H. James, has referred to. I was mobbed by the Tory members at the beginning of the Bill, but at the end all of them voted for it. (Laughter.) Well, one of the most intelligent Tory journals in London had an article on the North Riding Election, and they recommended the Tory candidate to the electors. And what was the main ground of the recommendation? It was that he was a gallant sportsman. (Laughter.) Well, I have no doubt he is. He comes of a very good stock, and I have no doubt he is a very excellent man. I have a great respect for sport

Various explanations were offered for the lapse: accurate reporting which somehow got past the sub-editor's blue pencil, a genuine mistake, or the spiteful action of a disgruntled employee.

Popular papers such as *The Porcupine* made great fun of the affair, but *Town Talk* was magisterial in its rebuke.

168

INDECENCY IN THE "TIMES" NEWSPAPER.

ON Monday morning week last considerable sensation was created throughout the Metropolis, and probably throughout the provinces also, by the publication in the *Times* newspaper of the most vile and filthy expression, to which we can do no more than allude. The horrible words were represented as having been spoken by the Right Hon. Sir William Harcourt. The editor of the *Times* has not vouchsafed an explanation as to how the leading journal became the medium for giving publicity to this filth. We presume that Sir William Harcourt did not give utterance to such expressions as the *Times* reports, and it may be taken for granted, therefore, that somebody engaged on the staff of that journal is responsible for the perpetration of a somewhat elaborate, if serious, practical joke. The *Times*, however, as we have said, offers no explanation of the manner in which it became the medium for the publication of filth, and it therefore rests with the Public Prosecutor to proceed against the publisher under Lord Campbell's Act for printing and selling an indecent paper. It is all very fine to say that the lewd paragraph is the result of a mistake or a trick; that may or may not be the case. If some dirty blackguard engaged on the printing staff of the *Times* has, after the proof sheets have been passed by the reader—for we cannot believe that any reader in full possession of his senses passed a proof containing such a vile insinuation on the Home Secretary—added the lines referred to while the type was on the "stone" ready to be made up, it behoves the proprietors of the *Times* to prosecute the scoundrel, and no doubt they could do so. If such a paragraph as graces the *Times* of January 23rd had by accident appeared in the columns of TOWN TALK, we might have sworn until we were black in the face that we were not responsible for its appearance without being believed. One editor may steal a horse, and another must not look over a hedge. What is it to do with the authorities under what circumstances filth is given to the world, or who publishes it? We say most distinctly that the contents of the *Times* of January 23rd render it entitled to the stigma of indecency, and that, therefore, the paper should have been seized, and the publisher been prosecuted forthwith. If the offensive matter found its way into print without his knowledge or sanction, no doubt the court would take that into consideration, but anyhow the truth would have come out, and the proprietors of other newspapers placed upon their guard. The publication of this garbage in the *Times* demonstrated one thing very clearly, and that was how delighted many thousands of people are to find something dirty in a newspaper. Before ten o'clock in the morning of the day on which the libel was published, everybody was talking about it with great glee, and copies of the *Times* were being paid for at the rate of five shillings each, and treasured by old and young men with as much eagerness as a miser treasures his ill-gotten gold. Before mid-day the filth had been reprinted on a small card and was almost publicly sold. The proprietors of the *Times* were said to have offered large sums of money for the restoration of copies of the paper, but dirty minded folks who had them were too delighted to possess them to think of bringing them to Printing House Square. We hope that the proprietors of the *Times* will in future exercise a little more care in printing the paper. This is not the first time, by any means, that dirt has been allowed to creep into the columns of the leading journal, but we hope that this will be the last.

TOWN TALK
February 4th, 1882

A Larger Circulation than all the Matrimonial Papers in the World combined

The Matrimonial Post

And Fashionable Marriage Advertiser.

And Matrimonial and Family Advice Bureau

INCORPORATED WITH "THE MARRIAGE POST AND FASHIONABLE MARRIAGE ADVISER."
(ESTABLISHED 1860.)

THE MATRIMONIAL AGENCY OF THE CIVILIZED WORLD.
WORLD-WIDE REPUTATION.

No. 1019   LONDON, FEBRUARY, 1952   PRICE 9d.

REGISTERED.

The Daily Liar.

NON-POLITICAL.   **NON-SENSICAL.**

[Entered at Stationers Hall.]   G.P.O.   COPYRIGHT

STARTLING BANK
SMASH AND GRAB RAID

From "THE DAILY LIAR" War Correspondent

Song, Words & Music.
By A. TOMCAT

Let us go for a walk, and a nice little talk,
On the nice...

The Good News paper

Sacramento
Edition

25¢

March 25, 1972   Vol. 3 No. 99
Published Fortnightly on Saturdays

A Little Knowledge That Acts
Is Worth Infinitely More Than
Much Knowledge That is Idle. — Gibran

"The World's Largest Selling Good News Newspaper"!

Boston to Buenos Aires

Grass Roots Diplomats, page 3

This Teacher's 'Love Project'
Is Shaking Up the Ghetto

CROSS-WORD PUZZLE No. 12.

Above:
An early Crossword Puzzle from
THE DAILY NEWS
December 23, 1924

Right:
DAILY MIRROR
July 1, 1970

Opposite:
THE MATRIMONIAL POST
No. 1019
February 1852
(438 x 290mm)

THE DAILY LIAR
(444 x 286mm)

THE GOOD NEWS PAPER
No. 99
March 25, 1972
(420 x 290mm)

Above:
DAILY NEWS, No. 24522, October 25, 1924 (600 x 435mm)
The Zinoviev Letter — proved to be a forgery.

DAILY EXPRESS, No. 12694, January 30, 1941 (600 x 410mm)
Proof-readers' nightmare: misprint in the front page headline.

THE TIMES, No. 61514, April 23, 1983 (600 x 395mm)
Editor's nightmare: 'Hitler's Diaries' turned out to be obvious fakes.

Daily Mirror

No. 5. NEWS BULLETIN. Price - One Penny.

Monday. May 10th. 1926.

GOVERNMENT'S POSITION.

STRIKE MUST BE CALLED OFF WITHOUT RESERVE, SAYS PREMIER.

Mr. Baldwin, in a broadcast message on Saturday said "The Government is fighting because while the coal negotiations were in progress the T.U.C. ordered a general strike presumably to try to force Parliament and the community to bend to its will. The Government is not fighting to lower the standard of living of the miners or of any other section of workers. My whole desire is to maintain the standard of living of every worker." The general strike he added, must be called off without reserve, the mining dispute could then be settled.

In another message the Premier stated that every man who remains at work or returns to work during the crisis will be protected from loss of Trade Union benefits or pensions.

MORE TRAINS TO-DAY.

Train services everywhere will be improved to-day. The L.M.S. state that station masters, clerks, signalmen, and other grades are returning and a greatly augmented service will be running. Practically the whole of the Southern Railway's Suburban electrified system is running a regular service. Many trains will run to the coast towns and intermediate stations. Only goods trains were run yesterday on the L.N.E.R. but an increased passenger service will operate to-day. L.N.E.R. clerks, still at work, have told their Union: "It does not matter one iota to the miners' cause whether we strike or not". Seventy-five stations on the underground are open.

300 L.G.O.C. BUSES RUNNING.

The L.G.O.C. state that they now have over 300 buses on four routes and 1,400 men have been trained as drivers and conductors.

COUNTRY QUIET.

The Home Secretary says the country generally is quiet. Following a disturbance in the Harrow Road, 18 arrests were made.

RUSSIANS' CHEQUE.

The T.U.C. state that a cheque has reached them from the All Russian Central Council of Trade Unions, Moscow. It ran into some thousands, but the T.U.C. decided to send a reply expressing appreciation but also their inability to accept the cheque and it has been returned.

PRINTERS CHANGE THEIR MINDS

Cambridge Branch of the National Union of Printing, Bookbinding & Paper Workers state they wish to return to work unconditionally.

OUR LEADING ARTICLE.

THE FIRST ROUND.

The first General Strike which this country has ever had to endure has now lasted nearly a week. The situation is still grave, but the first round is over and the life of the community has been maintained. We are warned by the Government that the climax is not yet reached. There is therefore need of all the coolness and courage that the nation can command in this unprecedented crisis of our history. But the assurance that such courage will not be lacking in all who inevitably suffer, in mind or body, through this attempt to paralyse the life of a great industrial community, is surely afforded by the wonderful spectacle of the endurance shown hitherto. The bulk of our people are uncomplaining. They stand solid behind the forces of law and order in a determination to "see it through"; as, so few years ago, they endured the daily spectacle of wounds and death rather than renounce the freedom that makes life worth while.

WANT TO GO BACK.

The entire clerical staff of the Manchester office of The Daily Mail has asked to be allowed to resume work to-day unconditionally.

THE PETS' MESSAGE.

Pip, Squeak and Wilfred are all quite well and through Uncle Dick, send their love to the children. Wilfred says "gug, gug" to his little friends.

ONLY PAY A PENNY!

Certain street hawkers are selling the Daily Mirror for 2d and 3d per copy. No more than one penny should be paid. The sellers are making more profit than before the Strike. The Daily Mirror and its illustrated supplement on Saturday reached a circulation of over 120,000 copies.

[illegible]

Fishermen are working ferry boats between Grimsby and Hull.

Seventy trams and over eighty buses are running in Edinburgh.

Shots were fired at Crewe at the driver of a train. No one was hurt.

Transport-workers in flour-milling industry have been ordered out at Liverpool, Birkenhead and Seacombe.

Messrs. Cadbury Ltd. state that all but 1,000 of their 3,500 men on strike will return to-day.

AUSTRALIANS 301 for 6.

The Australians scored 301 for 6 against Surrey at the Oval on Saturday.

All news messages are from Reuters and other agencies.

For latest news see over.

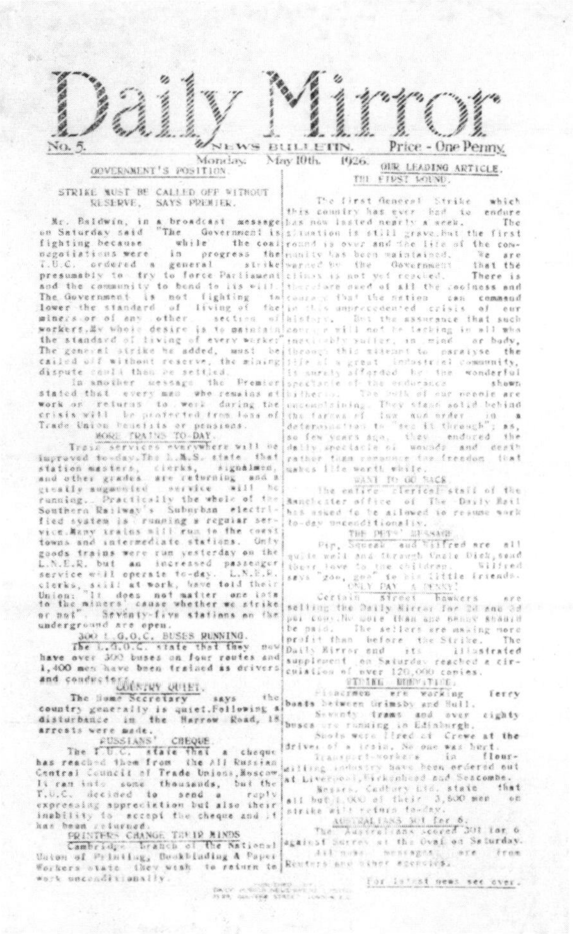

DAILY MIRROR,
News Bulletin
No. 5
May 10, 1926
(332 x 201mm)
One of the numerous hand printed special issues produced when Fleet Street printers joined the General Strike in 1926.

Right:
NU GINI TOKTOK
No. 45
August 8, 1963
(496 x 288mm)
New Guinea pidgin newspaper.
Note Volkswagen
advertisement: 'I-gat servis
I-gat spia' = 'I've got service:
I've got spares'.

Below:
Y CLORIANYDD
No. 3381
August 8, 1967
Welsh language newspaper.
headline = 'Report of the
Aberfan disaster puts blame on
the members of the Coal
Board'.

"Fake" newspapers also turn up, war time newspapers dropped behind enemy lines for instance, as well as deliberate fakes of early newspapers intended either to deceive, or produced simply as an educational aid. When newspapers go on strike there is usually an enterprising publisher prepared to step into the breach.

During the 1926 General Strike, in the absence of printers, the management of the national press, and many local papers, brought out their own newspapers on duplicators and small printing presses. The Trades Union Congress brought out its own *British Workman* and the Government the *British Gazette*. When Winston Churchill resigned for the last time as Prime Minister in 1955, the national press was on strike and it was left to local papers and independent strike-breaking tabloids such as the *Emergency Press* of 6 April to relay the news. When *The Times* was unpublished for almost a year because of a printers' strike in 1979, journalists produced *Not Yet The Times* with the headline: GOVERNMENT TO ABOLISH INCOME TAX. It was a spoof that became a collectors' item within days; other imitations jumped on the bandwagon including *The Times Challenger* and the *Sunday Times Reporter*.

The *Daily Liar* published by S. Burgess in the 1920s described itself as "Non-Political" and "Non-Sensical" and was full of jokes. In 1928 the *Daily Mail* produced an issue for 1 January 2000 for sale at the Ideal Home Exhibition projecting a vision of life seventy years on and printed in purple on yellow paper. In America in the 1970s was produced *The Good News Paper* committed to publishing only good news. When it closed down it was unable to notify its readers in advance.

There are plenty of quite genuine newspapers which are unusual. The *Matrimonial Post* designed solely to introduce potential partners; the

Right:
BRAILLE NEWS
SUMMARY
No. 17
September 23, 1960
(325 x 262mm)
Apart from the title page, the
text is entirely embossed in
Braille characters.

Below:
URDU TIMES GLASGOW
No. 3785
(505 x 380mm)

Overleaf:
SUNDAY TELEGRAPH
No. 645
July 8, 1973
(610 x 432mm)
Look, no pictures. The
engraves walk out.

NEWS CHRONICLE
No. 35648
October 17, 1960
(600 x 415mm)
The last issue.

THE EVENING NEWS
No. 12688
July 25, 1922
(600 x 415mm)
A headline that just does not
happen any more.

Braille News Summary for the blind; foreign and minority (Gaelic and Welsh) language newspapers published in Britain; newspapers printed on ocean liners or in prisons.

There are particular features of newspapers which have a collectable fascination. Crosswords appeared in America in 1913, and in Britain eleven years later. As the *Daily News* put it in December 1924, "Cross-word puzzles have become a national amusement, and the puzzle is to get enough of them." Duty stamps on nineteenth-century papers varied considerably from year to year and are collected in their own right. Strip cartoons which first appeared in the early twentieth century have their own devotees.

An unusual approach to collecting, but one which will have its own personal appeal, is to keep newspapers published on the birth-day of a child, and on subsequent birthdays, preferably evening papers reporting the events of the day.

First and last issues are a specific, and difficult, area to collect. "Number One" of any newspaper is probably easier to find, bearing in mind that many have been reprinted, because the print-runs are usually large, and they tend to have been kept as curiosities. Last issues often disappear into dustbins before many people have realised that the newspaper has folded or been amalgamated with another. The *News Chronicle* in its 35,648th issue of 17 October 1960 gave a cryptic hint to its readers that all might not be well: "It would be unwise to say anything at the moment" commented the Managing Director. It did not appear again.

The odd and unusual, the eccentric and out-of-the-way have their own momentary interest, but there are very few George Ives to record them for future reference.

Five miniature newspapers reprinted by the proprietors for publicity purposes. (Ranging in size from 65 x 45mm to 120 x 86mm.)

179

The Times.

Number 6572.   LONDON, THURSDAY, NOVEMBER 7, 1805.   **Price 6d.**

EUROPEAN MUSEUM.

GERRARD DOW'S celebrated PIC-
TURE of the DOUBLE SURPRISE is
arrived at the above National Gallery. The Nobility and Gentry who wish to become subscribers
for the ensuing season are requested to be early in
their application, as the Books will soon be closed.

J. WILSON, Manager.
Hours from 12 till 4. Admission 1s.

WEST INDIA DOCK COMPANY.

THE COURT of DIRECTORS of
the WEST INDIA DOCK COMPANY do
hereby give notice that a CALL of 25l. per Cent. is
required to be paid into the hands of Messrs. Smith,
Payne and Smith, Mansion House Street, on or before Thursday, the 5th day of December next, being
the third instalment on the last West India Dock
additional subscription of 100,000.

By order of the Court of Directors.
THOS. MARKHAM, Sec.
West India Dock House, 6th Nov., 1805.

This day is published

A PORTRAIT of LORD NELSON,
from a picture painted by J. Hoppner, R.A.
for the Royal Highness the Prince of Wales.
To be had of Messrs Colnaghi, Cockspur Street,
Haymarket, and at the Engraver's, 63 Great Russell
Street, Bloomsbury.

WANTED to RENT for three months,
a small DWELLING HOUSE, ready fur-
nished, in an airy situation, suitable for the recep-
tion of a genteel family, within half an hour's walk
West of the Royal Exchange.

LOST, an OLD POINTER DOG,
White, with red spots, answers to the name of
BASTO, almost blind. One guinea given. Any
person bringing the said Dog to No. 125, Swallow
Street, Foulsmith, shall receive ONE GUINEA Re-
ward, and reasonable expenses paid.

MODERN TOWN COACH and ex-
cellent HARNESS,—to be SOLD, an excel-

IRSH LINENS, FRENCH CAM-
BRICS, &c., wholesale and retail, at No. 15,
Oxford-street, corner of Berner's-street. W. M.
Cooper has just received several bales of Irish
linens particularly cheap; several bales of French
cambrics very fine at 50s. the price upwards. A
large quantity of blankets, counterpanes, Marseilles
quilts, bed furniture, several bales of damask and
diaper table linen, with napkins to match, dimities
of every description very cheap; stout India calico,
full wide, at 13d. and 14d. per yard, with a variety of other articles. As a low wholesale price is
invariably asked, (being much under the regular
price,) no abatement is ever made.

THE THREE PIGEONS, 296, Holborn, opposite Brownlow-street.—BETTS,
For Manufacturers, begs leave to inform the
Ladies and the Public in General, that he has now
ready for their inspection a very extensive AS-
SORTMENT of MUFFS, TIPPETS, TRIM-
MINGS for PELISSES, &c. &c., all of his own
manufacture, very considerably under the usual
prices.—J. B. having purchased a large quantity of
Skins at the last March sales remarkably low, and
has had them made up immediately under his own
inspection, is able to sell full 30 per cent. lower than
the trade in general. Velvets for Spencers and pelisses from 7s. per yard upwards. Gloves 1s. per pair
upwards; real white Silk Handkerchiefs 6s. each.
Lace and Haberdashery remarkably cheap. A
large assortment of Velvet Hats and Bonnets of all
descriptions and prices.

THE ORIGINAL MANUFAC-
TORY.—The frequent attempts to mislead
the Public induces BUTLER to request the Public
to be particular as to the house. The PATENT
BRONZE and DINING TABLES.

CHILBLAINS are prevented from
breaking, and their tormenting itching instantly removed, by WHITEHEAD'S ESSENCE
of MUSTARD.

The Times.

NUMBER 6572.   LONDON, THURSDAY, NOVEMBER 7, 1805.   **PRICE SIXPENCE.**

The LONDON GAZETTE EXTRAORDINARY.
WEDNESDAY, Nov 6, 1805.

ADMIRALTY-OFFICE, Nov. 6.

Dispatches, of which the following are Copies,
were received at the Admiralty this day, at one
o'clock A.M. from Vice-Admiral Collingwood,
Commander in Chief of his Majesty's ships and
vessels off Cadiz:—

SIR,   Euryalus, off Cape Trafalgar, Oct. 22, 1805.

The ever-to-be-lamented death of Vice-Admiral
Lord Viscount Nelson, who, in the late conflict
with the enemy, fell in the hour of victory, leaves
to me the duty of informing my Lords Commissioners of the Admiralty, that on the 19th instant,
it was communicated to the Commander in Chief,
from the ships watching the motions of the enemy
in Cadiz, that the Combined Fleet had put to sea;
as they sailed with light winds westerly, his Lordship concluded their destination was the Mediterranean, and immediately made all sail for the
Streights' entrance, with the British Squadron, consisting of twenty-seven ships, three of them sixty-
fours, where his Lordship was informed, by Captain Blackwood (whose vigilance in watching, and
giving notice of the enemy's movements, has been
highly meritorious), that they had not yet passed
the Streights.

On Monday the 21st instant, at day-light, when
Cape Trafalgar bore E. by S. about seven leagues,
the enemy was discovered six or seven miles to
the Eastward; the wind about West, and very light;
the Commander in Chief immediately made the sig-
nal for the fleet to bear up in two columns, as they
are formed in order of sailing; a mode of attack his
Lordship had previously directed, to avoid the in-
convenience and delay in forming a line of battle
in the usual manner. The enemy's line consisted
of thirty-three ships (of which eighteen were
French, and fifteen Spanish), commanded in Chief by
Admiral Villeneuve: the Spaniards, under the direction of Gravina, were, with their heads to the
Northward, and formed their line of battle with
great closeness and correctness; but as the mode of
attack was unusual, so the structure of their line
was new; it formed a crescent, conveying to her

in their country's service, all deserve that their
high merits should stand recorded; and never was
high merit more conspicuous than in the battle I
have described.

The Achille (a French 74), after having sur-
rendered, by some mismanagement of the French-
men, took fire and blew up; two hundred of her
men were saved by the Tenders.

A circumstance occurred during the action,
which so strongly marks the invincible spirit of
British seamen, when engaging the enemies of their
country, that I cannot resist the pleasure I have in
making it known to their Lordships; the Teme-
raire was boarded by accident, or design, by a
French ship on one side, and a Spaniard on the
other; the contest was vigorous, but, in the end,
the Combined Englishmen were sure from the poop,
and the British hoisted in their places.

Such a battle could not be fought without sus-
taining a great loss of men. I have not only to
lament, in common with the British Navy, and the
British Nation, in the fall of the Commander in
Chief, the loss of a Hero, whose name will be im-
mortal, and his memory ever dear to his country;
but my heart is rent with the most poignant grief for
the death of a friend, to whom, by many years in-
timacy, and a perfect knowledge of the virtues of
his mind, which inspired ideas superior to the common rigor of men, I was bound by the strongest ties
of affection; a grief to which even the glorious occasion in which he fell, does not bring the consolation which, perhaps, it ought: his Lordship received a musket ball in his left breast, about the
middle of the action, and sent an Officer to me immediately with his last farewell; and soon after
expired.

I have also to lament the loss of those excellent
Officers, Captains Duff, of the Mars, and Cooke, of
the Bellerophon; I have yet heard of none others.

I fear the numbers that have fallen will be found
very great, when the returns come to me; but it
having blown a gale of wind ever since the action,
I have not yet had it in my power to collect any
reports from the ships.

The Royal Sovereign having lost her masts, ex-

under my command, for their conduct on that day; but more
can I find language to express my sentiments of the valour and
skill which were displayed by the Officers, the Seamen, and
Marines in the battle with the enemy. were every individual
appeared an Hero, on whom the Glory of his Country de-
pended; the attack was irresistible, and the issue of it added to
the page of Naval Annals a brilliant instance of what Britons
can do, when they King and their Country need their service.

To the Right Honourable Rear-Admiral the Earl of Northesk,
to the Captains, Officers, and Seamen and to the Officers, Non-
commissioned Officers, and Privates of the Royal Marines, I
beg to give my sincere and hearty thanks for their highly meritorious conduct, both in the action, and in their zeal and ala-
crity in bringing the captured ships out from the perilous situation in which they were afterwards exposed, among the shoals
of Trafalgar, in boisterous weather.

And I desire that the respective Captains will be pleased to
communicate to the Officers, Seamen, and Royal Marines, that
public testimony of my high approbation of their conduct, and
my thanks for it.   (Signed)   C. COLLINGWOOD.
To the Right Honourable Rear-Admiral the Earl of Northesk,
and the respective Captains and Commanders.

GENERAL ORDER.

The Almighty God, whose arm is strength, having of his
great mercy been pleased to crown the exertion of his Majesty's
fleet with success, in giving them a complete victory over their
enemies, on the of this month: and that all make and thanks-
giving may be offered up to the Throne of Grace for the great
benefits to our country and to mankind.

I have, &c.

N. B. The fleet having been dispersed by a gale
of wind, no day has yet been able to be appointed
for the above purpose.

SIR,   Euryalus, off Cadiz, Oct. 24. 1805.

In my letter of the 22d, I detailed to you, for the
information of my Lords Commissioners of the
Admiralty, the proceedings of his Majesty's squadron on the day of the action, and that preceding
it, since which I have had a continued series of
misfortunes; but they are of a kind that human
prudence could not possibly provide against, or
my skill prevent.

On the 22d, in the morning, a strong southerly
wind blew, with squally weather, which, however,

FAKES, FORGERIES AND REPRINTS

The history of the newspaper has thrown up its fair share of fakes, forgeries and reprints which are confusing to the unwary, even if the original intention was not to deceive.

The first-ever British newspaper was, for a period, accepted as the *English Mercurie*. This was supposed to have been published by Queen Elizabeth I's government just before the threat of invasion from the Spanish Armada in 1588, and copies were brought to the attention of the public, apparently for the first time, in 1794 by a Mr Chalmers writing in the *Gentleman's Magazine*. Seven numbers, four in manuscript and three set in type, were revealed. No. 1 for 23 July 1588 contained advices from Sir Francis Wallsingham reporting the movements of the Armada.

The papers were adjudged "transparent forgeries" in 1839 by Thomas Watts of the British Museum in "A Letter to Antonio Panizzi Esq. . . . on the Reputed Earliest Printed Newspaper, *The English Mercurie*". Watts deduced it to be a fake on at least five counts:

1. The printed papers used type dating from about 1716.
2. Two of the written numbers are the originals, in modern spelling, of the printed copies which have been set in badly imitated antique spelling, e.g. "storme" for "storm".
3. The handwriting is of as modern a character as the type.
4. They are made up of a confusion of dates and circumstances that could hardly have occurred had they been written at the time represented.
5. The paper on which the manuscript is written bears the watermark of the royal arms and initial G.R.

It took "not two minutes" for Watts to realise a forgery which was accepted for over forty years as genuine and, as he pointed out, "had the writers who so readily adopted Chalmer's statements . . . looked at the paper they were writing about, (the forgery) must have been detected long before".

Opposite:
THE TIMES
No. 6572
November 7, 1805
Top copy is a FAKE; bottom copy is a facsimile of the original.

181

Nevertheless, these fakes can still be seen in the Manuscripts Department of the British Library. Perhaps the best known example of newspaper forgery has been *The Times* of 7 November 1805 which contained Vice-Admiral Collingwood's famous dispatch reporting the death of Nelson. Annual celebrations to commemorate the Battle of Trafalgar were taken over in 1896 by the Navy League. On 21 October that year, Trafalgar Square was beginning to fill up as early as 7 am; banners, laurels and portraits decorated every corner and hawkers did a brisk trade throughout the day in pamphlets and books, including copies of *The Times* 1805. A few days after the celebrations, *The Times* felt it necessary to carry a paragraph warning readers that the papers sold on that day were not, in fact, genuine.

Such warnings have been given by the paper at fairly frequent intervals ever since. In 1932 a small article was headed: "Famous Issues of *The Times*. Reprints and Spurious Copies".

> As one consequence of the change in type of *The Times* many alleged copies of early issues have been offered to us. We think it necessary to state that in the majority of cases these are not what they profess to be.

The article refers specifically to the 1805 issue. Thousands have been sent to the paper over the years, but none have proved genuine. As the circulation in 1805 was only about 2,500, this is not surprising. The history of the "forgeries", and the legitimate reproductions produced by *The Times* itself, was outlined in the paper in 1971:

> On their first appearance in the 1880s, the spurious copies were facsimiles, but later jobbing printers grew careless (and greedy) and gradually appalling attempts at verisimilitude were being printed and hawked around. Some years ago a printer even telephoned Printing House Square *(then*

182

home of The Times) to ask for discount terms for a large order for the official reprint. He said he wanted to sell them on 21 October, as his plates had been destroyed in the Blitz. To those in Printing House Square, the detection of the majority of spurious copies is a simple matter. If there are four columns of advertising on the front cover, it can be rejected immediately. A genuine specimen carries advertisements only on column one, and the Admiralty dispatch begins in the adjoining column. If the price is printed "6d" the copy is spurious — the original has "sixpence".

The most blatant forgery is one that cannibalises two issues of *The Times* and contains news of the victory and also a poem on the death of Nelson. The poem, in fact, did not appear on 7 November, but on 7 December 1805. In theory, any copy which does not bear the newspaper duty stamp cannot be genuine, but it is known that sometimes sheets were missed in the stamping process or that the stamp might have been cropped off in binding into a volume.

The early counterfeits are easy to distinguish from the original because of changes in type, and variations in the coat-of-arms in the masthead.

THE TIMES

Art: Seige, Bricksand Politics
by Bernard Levin,
page 3

The fight goes on against anarchy and extravagance

'The Times' is back after a nine month stand against the uncontrolled power of the trade unions. The 'Sunday Times' and the three supplements will reappear soon. Lord Thomson of Fleet, President of Times Newspapers said that there is no question of a defeat in his decision to reopen the newspaper.

A truly heroic stand

Robot whales resolve cetacean neurosis

Arab groups taking over British industries

President Carter resigns from the White House

Rhodesia: Government coalition likely to collapse

Spurious issue of THE TIMES, No. 60473, July 1979 (630 x 420mm)
While the genuine Times *is away, the journalists will play.*

184

With later imitations reproduced directly from the original, paper quality is the guide. Modern reprints have usually been printed on card, or heavy quality smooth paper, rather than the original handmade paper in which the type is quite heavily impressed.

A little earlier than the first *Times* reprints, a series of famous early newspapers was brought out entitled "Pigott's Portfolio". The titles included *The Gazette* No. 432 September 1658, the *English Mercurie* 23 July 1588 (a reprint of a forgery!), the *Weekly Newes* No. 19 for January 1606, the *Intelligencer* No. 288 January-February 1648, the *Newes* No. 52 for 6 July 1665 and the *London Gazette* September 1666.

The enterprising "gentleman" who produced these reprints was Richard Pigott, Irish journalist and forger. When his own paper the *Irishman* was in financial difficulties in 1865, he supplemented his income by selling pornographic pictures, but he is best remembered for his part in the Parnell Letters Scandal of 1887 when he forged letters purporting to have been written by Charles Parnell, the Irish Home Rule leader, implicating him in the Phoenix Park Murders. Pigott sold the letters to *The Times* which was duped into printing them as originals.

It seems amazing that anyone should be taken in by Pigott's attempts at newspaper "forgery". The type to reprint the papers was newly set up, so that there are striking differences from the originals. Type faces of the 1880s were, of course, substantialy different from those of two centuries earlier and the paper used by Pigott of much poorer quality, and yet, the reprint of the *Newes*, reporting the Great Plague of London, has been used as an illustration of the original in a book on newspaper history as recently as 1964.

Offset printing makes the reproduction of originals much easier. A full-page photograph of

an original can quickly be transferred on to a plate and reproduced in thousands, in exactly the same way that most local newspapers are printed today. This technology has been effectively exploited by several reprint series, particularly *Great Newspapers Reprinted* and *The War Papers* brought out in the 1970s. Concentrating mainly on reproducing historical newspapers of the twentieth century in their entirety, the end product is often difficult to tell from the original except for occasional fading of the type where the photography has failed to pick up all the detail on a page, or because the size of a page has been slightly altered to accommodate the most convenient modern paper size available. Other indications of the differrence between original and reproduction are the failure to print "stop press" boxes in the original red or blue and, in one example, the filling in of a puzzle by an orignal reader which has been faithfully reprinted in every copy.

Issues in these series, now completed, sold orignally for a few pence a time but are already collectors items in their own right — as reproductions. However, a *Comics of World War I* special issue of *Great Newspapers Reprinted* which included six comics and sold at 20p, has since found its way on to the "genuine" or, rather, forgery, market; each separate comic selling for pounds as an original.

Similar enterprises to *Great Newspapers Reprinted* sprang up in other countries in the mid 1970s. In Germany these were printed on heavy gloss paper which could never be confused with the original. In New Zealand a small educational company followed the idea with early antipodean newspapers.

In America reprints have largely been restricted to front pages, often bound up into large folio books. An example of a complete reprint is from Tombstone, Arizona; The *Tombstone Epitaph* of Thursday 27 October 1881. An artificially browned paper, in which the main story is the

"Shoot-out at O.K. Corral" in which three men were "hurled into eternity in the duration of a moment" by Marshall Wyatt Earp and Doc Holliday. On the back page a section of text is missing in which a note is added: "The original copy of the issue in which this item appeared was clipped at this point". Also in America, Civil War newspaper reprints are sold in packs at the supermarket.

Newspaper companies themselves are very conscious of their own past history. A common feature of long-established papers is the regular reprinting of snippets of news from twenty-five, fifty or a hundred years ago. The opportunity presented by a centenary or anniversary is often taken to reprint first or early issues, a publicity gimmick which started in the nineteenth century when everyone from the *Plymouth and Dock Telegraph* to the *Northampton Mercury* tried the idea. A number of newspapers have sponsored reprints; for a while the *Northern Echo* included an historical issue free every month; the *Birmingham Post* has reproduced several early isues, and of course, *The Times*. Newspaper companies also produce miniature editions for advertising purposes. One American collector has amassed an almost unbelievable 16,000 of these mini-papers.

From time to time, independent companies offer to supply reprinted front pages for a particular date — a birthday or wedding. At the British Library Newspaper Library there are facilities for Readers to have any page copied, though this can take some time. Readers can also photograph pages themselves by arrangement although, without the right equipment, the results are unlikely to be satisfactory.

The purist collector may dismiss a reprint in the same way as he or she would dismiss a less than perfect original. At the same time reprints may be the only way that newspaper rarities can be obtained in any concrete form.

Fakes, forgeries and reprints are also collectable in their own right.

THE
INTELLIGENCER.
A PERFECT DIURNAL

OF SOME

PASSAGES IN PARLIAMENT,

And the Daily Proceedin *Army under His·Excellency*
fax.

FROM MUNDAY, THE AY, THE 5TH OF FEB., 1648.
Collected fr *he correctly informed.*
Printed by E. G.   OAKE, and are so sold at their

THE
Englifh Mercurie.
Publifhed by AUTHORITIE.
For the Prevention of falfe Reportes.

Whitehall, July 23d, 1588.

EARLIE this Morninge arrived a Meſſenger at Sir Francis Walſinghams Office, with Letters of the 22d from the Lorde High Admirall; advertiſing, that aboute the 26th of his Infant Cap. Fleming, who had beene ordered to cruize in the Chops of the Channel, for Diſcoverye, brought Advice into Plymouth, that he had deſcried the Meſk-Royal, neare the Lizard, making for the Channell ...

mbers comming into
voted, That such
md of settling a
the future.

of c.
pared
preserv\
ready, an
thereof.

 This day
grants, patents,
of England and l.

  Be it enacted by
equity, and in all writ,
fines, recoveries, exemp.
kingdom of England and l.
title, and treats of *Custodes,*

s and letters
ld be pre-
keep and
scripts
bate

tho
e, stile,
d the date

PRESERVATION OF NEWSPAPERS

Newspaper offices keep "file" copies of their back issues bound up in volumes.

The *News of the World*, for instance, keeps its gigantic folios, stretching back to 1843, in a basement room next to the boiler house. Everything is covered with a thick layer of dust; several of the volumes are falling apart. Turning the pages, corners and edges flake off, the paper tears.

At the *Express*, anyone searching out the papers that covered the R101 disaster, for instance, will find the issue of the *Sunday Express* which played an important part in newspaper history in a terrible state. The front page is missing, the rest of the issue torn and frayed. The front page has, in fact, been framed and put on a wall. The *Daily Express* for the following Monday is in another file; the boards are off the volume and the first few issues almost non-existent.

The *Daily Sketch*, unusually, maintained a file which included copies of all *editions* of the *Sketch* that were published — four or five a day. Most newspapers have kept only the final edition for each day. After the merger with the *Daily Mail* these unique files were sold off to make space. Luckily, they found their way into the British Library.

Such lack of concern for back issues is a surprising contrast with the way in which newspapers like to take every opportunity to "puff" their own history. At the same time, even a great newspaper library like that of the British Library at Colindale, north London has problems with preservation. These are exacerbated by the amount of handling they receive from readers. Even with the utmost care in turning pages, paper tends to break up, sometimes at the merest touch.

Quality of paper used for newsprint has varied considerably over the centuries. Until the beginning of the nineteenth century, all paper was hand-made and limited in size by the mould. Paper-making machinery was introduced into

Opposite:
THE INTELLIGENCER
(260 x 185mm)

THE ENGLISH MERCURIE
(250 x 185mm)
Two titles in "Piggott's Portfolio" of reprints, published in the 1880's.

189

England in 1803, and into America in 1827. Until the 1870s paper was made from linen and cotton "rag" which produced excellent paper, but became difficult to obtain in sufficient quantity. Rag paper, preserved in a binding, unfolded and kept away from damp, is as good today as when it was first made.

Breakthrough to using wood pulp solved the crisis of paper shortage, but meant lower quality. The worst period for paper quality was the late nineteenth to early twentieth century; in the search for cheapness, the results have not stood the test of time. The paper used then is often so poor that it turns brown and brittle under almost any conditions.

During and after World War II, paper shortage was reflected in thinness and low quality of newsprint. The inability of modern newspapers to withstand age is argued by some collectors as a reason for not collecting them at all. In fact, a reasonable amount of care can keep deterioration to a minimum.

Light, heat and humidity are the three main enemies to paper preservation. Sunlight is the most effective destroyer of paper. Discoloration of a newspaper left on a window ledge or back shelf of a car for a week testifies to this. The answer is obvious; keep all newspapers away from bright light, either natural or artificial.

An even temperature and a not-too-dry atmosphere are important. On the one hand do not store paper in an outhouse or attic where there is a possibility of water penetration, or a basement which is damp and musty; on the other, use a room without central heating, unless a humidifier is also used. Air-conditioning provides the most controlled environment. A small amount of care to avoid the excesses of light, heat and humidity is the basic necessity.

Ideal storage is in a dry shelved cupboard with doors. The shelves must be wide enough to take newspapers flat out. Fold the newspapers as little as possible — it is along folds that brittleness begins. Separate copies by placing them in card folders or acetate bags clearly labelled for easy reference. File smaller newspapers in transparent pocket folders.

If the paper has reached a state of breaking up, the whole page can be treated with a coat of clear size. Large tears must be mended with Japanese tissue and a water-based glue. Do not use sellotape; after only a matter of months this will peel off leaving a heavy irremovable brown stain.

Newspapers which have accumulated dust and dirt can be cleaned up substantially by simply rubbing off with clean pieces of soft white bread.

Bound volumes of newspapers, usually before 1900, can still be found. If a volume, or volumes, contain a complete or substantial run it is not advisable to "break" them in order to extract individual issues, in the same way that a book should not be broken in order to extract maps or illustrations. However, an odd volume of newspapers is really a collection of individual issues, each separately published, and can be compared with a collection of individually published pamphlets which have been bound together for the convenience of a previous owner. If the decision is to break a volume, do it with the greatest care so that the paper is not torn in the process. Use a sharp Stanley knife to remove the boards and slowly go through cutting the sewing down the spine. Remove each issue as it comes free from the binding.

On the other hand, a special collection of related newspapers may require binding up into a volume. This is a job that should be tackled only by a professional bookbinder. A reputable antiquarian bookseller can arrange for this to be done. The best way of approaching this is to have a binding made with stubs to which the newspaper can be attached.

Do not make holes for filing in looseleaf folders or use spring-clips which will almost certainly cause damage.

A collection must be kept in reasonable order. Without it, finding particular isues when required will be impossible. Keep a simple card index with cross-references to each section. Make a system and stick to it.

ACQUISITION

BUILDING A COLLECTION

Buying and selling old newspapers has traditionally been part of the antiquarian and second-hand book trade. In the past, this has meant buying and selling volumes of pre-1900 newspapers or earlier individually bound newsbooks.

As the quantity of bound volumes decreases and the interest in collecting newspapers increases, more booksellers are dealing in individual unbound, or disbound, issues and of more recent vintage. And, as part of the general trend in bookselling towards greater specialisation, a number of dealers have emerged as specialising only in newspapers and periodicals.

Of these, the majority sell by post, either by quoting directly to customers or by producing catalogues or lists sent free on request. Such catalogues, more than anything else, give an idea of current prices "in the trade". There are also a handful of dealers who have shop or office premises open to the public.

The level of trading is very small compared with the second-hand book trade and as a result, dealers and collectors are well known to each other. Although some American dealers have attempted to "market" old newspapers by advertising through large circulation magazines at vastly inflated prices, buying and selling retains the personal touch of the antiquarian book world.

Many dealers in antiquarian and second-hand books also sell by mail order, and occasionally include volumes or individual copies of newspapers in their catalogues.

The general second-hand bookshop is the most likely place to find bargains; like many bric-a-brac and junk shops, they usually keep a pile or box of newspapers and magazines.

Book Fairs, where booksellers from all over the country set up their stalls for one or two days, are regularly held in London and provincial centres. There are also specialist Ephemera Fairs, where dealers exhibiting deal almost exclusively in throw-awayable printed material from the past, including newspapers.

193

The best approach is to discover the booksellers in the area where you live; visit each of them and tell them exactly what your interest is. Even better, write down what you are looking for, together with your name and address. Many booksellers will search on behalf of customers. Ask a dealer with whom you get along well to advertise through the trade magazines for your "wants".

Auctions are a possible source of supply, particularly for newsbooks and early newspapers, although there are few specialist sales. Bound volumes often reach high prices — though measured in terms of the number of issues in each they may well be relatively cheap.

Collectors can also use the press to advertise their wants. *Exchange and Mart* has a regular column for newspaper and magazine collectors, and an advertisement in a local paper is worth trying.

For background research, a select bibliography of books on newspaper history is included in this volume. The best place in the British Isles for looking at original newspapers is the British Library Newspaper Library at Colindale, north London. All provincial newspapers, and London newspapers published after 1800 are housed here; all London newspapers published before that date are in the British Library, Bloomsbury, London WC1 and based on the Burney Collection. To use both libraries it is necessary to obtain a Reader's ticket. The Welsh National Library at Aberystwyth and the Scottish National Library in Edinburgh both have large collections available for reference.

Most local libraries keep files of local newspapers, and of at least one national newspaper, usually *The Times*. The best public reference library for information on newspapers is the St Bride Printing Library, just off Fleet Street in the City of London.

There have been several attempts by newspaper collectors to form clubs. These have tended to rely on the efforts of one or two people to produce regular news-letters, and none of them has survived. However, in 1982, the latest venture, the Newspaper Collectors Club, was launched in Tewkesbury, Gloucestershire in tandem with the opening of the Museum of Newspapers and Caricature.

NEWSPAPER LIBRARIES AND COLLECTIONS

BRITISH LIBRARY
Great Russell Street, London WC1.
The national collection of London newspapers published up to 1800, including the Burney Collection. Readers ticket required.

BRITISH LIBRARY NEWSPAPER LIBRARY
Colindale Avenue, London NW9 5HE.
The national collection of newspapers published outside London, and London newspapers 1801 to the present day. The library publishes a regular newsletter for those interested in newspaper librarianship. Readers ticket required.

NATIONAL LIBRARY OF SCOTLAND
George IV Bridge, Edinburgh.
The library has a large collection of Scottish newspapers.

NATIONAL LIBRARY OF WALES
Aberystwyth, Dyfed SY23 3BU.
The library has a large collection of Welsh newspapers and microfilm copies.

ST. BRIDE PRINTING LIBRARY
St. Bride Institute, Bride Lane, Fleet Street, London EC4.
A public library with an exceptional collection of books relating to the history of the press.

INTERNATIONALES ZEITUNGSMUSEUM DER STADT AACHEN (Aachen Newspaper Museum)
Ponststrasse 13, Aachen, West Germany.

MUSEUM OF NEWSPAPERS AND CARICATURE
39 Church Street, Tewkesbury, Gloucestershire.
Proprietor: K. Tombs.
A small independent museum with displays of newspapers covering the events of British history, and illustrating the development of the press. Mr Tombs has also established the Newspaper Collectors Club. Museum open Tues-Sat 10am-1pm, 2pm-5.30pm.

HISTORICAL NEWSPAPER SERVICE
8 Monks Avenue, New Barnet, Hertfordshire. Tel: 01 440 3159.
Proprietor: John Frost.
Britain's largest private collection of over 25,000 newspapers, 1630 to the present day, but mainly 20th century. Individual issues are loaned out, for a fee, mainly to television, radio, theatre and the press.

DEALERS IN NEWSPAPERS

ANTIQUE NEWS
29 Parkfield Road, Stourbridge, West Midlands.
Proprietor: Mr Selby
17th & 18th century Newspapers; also early documents. Mail order.

BARBICAN BOOKSHOP
24 Fossgate, York YO1 2TA. Tel: 0904 53643
Director: H. L. Bingham
Bound volumes of newspapers and magazines. Shop, 9.00am-5.30pm.

DAVID GODFREY'S OLD NEWSPAPER SHOP
37 Kinnerton Street, London SW1X 8ED. Tel: 01-235 7788
Newspapers 1665 to present day. Individual issues arranged according to particular content. Shop 11.30am-5.30pm Mon-Fri.

DICKINSON, R. J.
46 St. Monica Grove, Durham City DH1 4AT
Collector and dealer. Bookstall at Durham New Market.

FROGNAL RARE BOOKS
18 Cecil Court, London WC2. Tel: 01-240 2815
Runs of early newspapers, books on newspapers, especially relating to liberty of the press.

JARNDYCE ANTIQUARIAN BOOKSELLERS
68 Neal Street, Covent Garden, London WC2. Tel: 01-836 9182 or 01-267 2307
Partners: Brian Lake & Janet Nassau
Occasional lists of newspapers 17th century-20th century and books on newspaper history.

HAROLD LANDRY
19 Tanza Road, London NW3 2UA. Tel: 01-435 8354
Bound volumes of periodicals and newspapers. Mail order.

MESSENGERS
7 Eldertree Gardens, Exeter, Devon EX4 4DE. Tel: 0392 213540
Proprietor: Barrie Evans
Postal auction catalogues of ephemera which include individual issues of newspapers, 3 issues a year to subscribers.

L. M. C. NIERYNCK
Verdilaan 85, 4384 LD Vlissingen, The Netherlands. Tel: 01184 70172
Newspapers 17th century-19th century. Mail order catalogues.

ORIGINAL AND RARE NEWSPAPER CO.
Unit 46, Covent Garden Market, London WC2. Tel: 01-379 7779
Proprietor: Robert Heron
Individual issues of newspapers 1620-1855. Gallery & office. ANNIVERSARY PRESS at the same address sells issues of several titles for particular dates 1890-1980.

PETER MURRAY HILL LTD.
35 North Hill, Highgate, London N6. Tel: 01-340 6959
Director: Martin Hamlyn
Bound volumes of newspapers 17th century-early 19th century. Occasional mail order catalogues.

SPREAD EAGLE ANTIQUES
8 Nevada Street, Greenwich, London SE10. Tel: 01 692 1618 or 01 858 9713
Proprietors: R. F. & A. Moy
Newspapers and magazines 18th century-20th century, especially Royal issues. Shop.

TILLEY'S BOOKSHOP
29/31 South Street, New Whittington, Chesterfield, Derbyshire S43 2AA. Tel: 0246 473047
Newspaper and comics 1790s — present day. Shop & mail order.

YESTERDAY'S NEWS
43 Dundonald Road, Colwyn Bay, Clwyd, North Wales LI29 7RE. Tel: 0492 31195
Proprietor: Ed Jones
Newspapers 1730s-20th century, also periodicals and ephemera. Issues supplied for particular dates. Large stock may be viewed by appointment.

YESTERDAY'S PAPER
4a Colliergate, York. Tel: 0904 642584
Dealers in a wide range of printed ephemera, including newspapers. Shop.

Consult the *Directory of Dealers in Secondhand and Antiquarian Books in the British Isles* (Sheppard Press) for a comprehensive listing of booksellers who may stock newspapers from time to time. The *Directory* also lists auction houses which hold book sales.

COLLECTORS' AND DEALERS' ASSOCIATIONS

NEWSPAPER COLLECTORS CLUB
39 Church Street, Tewkesbury, Gloucestershire
(See *Museum of Newspapers* listed under *LIB-RARIES.*)

THE EPHEMERA SOCIETY
12 Fitzroy Square, London W1P 5HQ. Tel: 01 387 7723
Organises meetings and fairs for anyone interested in printed ephemera, including newspapers & magazines. Publishes *The Ephemerist.*

PROVINCIAL BOOKSELLERS FAIRS ASSOCIATION
60-61 Quarry Street, Guildford, Surrey. Tel: 0483 572528
Booksellers' association which organises book fairs throughout Britain; provides a list of members with their specialities, and dates of forthcoming fairs, on request.

ANTIQUARIAN BOOKSELLERS ASSOCIATION (INT.)
154 Buckingham Palace Road, London SW1. Tel: 01 730 9273
Booksellers' association; provides a list of members on request.

PRINCIPAL LONDON BOOK AUCTION ROOMS

BLOOMSBURY BOOK AUCTIONS
6 Bedford Square, London WC1. Tel: 01-636 1945.

CHRISTIE'S
8 King Street, London SW1. Tel: 01-839 9060.
(Also at: 85 Old Brompton Road, London SW7. Tel: 01-581 2231).

PHILLIPS'
7 Blenheim Street, London W1. Tel: 01-409 3193

SOTHEBY'S
Bloomfield Place, New Bond Street, London W1. Tel: 01-493 8080.

BIBLIOGRAPHY

ALLEN, R. & FROST, J., *Daily Mirror* (Patrick Stephens 1981).

ALLEN, R. & FROST, J., *Voice of Britain. The Inside Story of the Daily Express* (Patrick Stephens 1983).

ANDREWS, Alexander, *The History of British Journalism* (Richard Bentley 1859). One of the earliest works on newspaper history.

ANGLO, M., *Service Newspapers of the Second World War* (Jupiter 1977).

ATKINSON, Frank, *The English Newspaper since 1900* (Library Association 1960). A detailed bibliography of books about modern newspapers.

AYERST, David, *Guardian. Biography of a Newspaper* (Collins 1971).

BAYNES, Ken, etc. *Scoop, Scandal and Strife, A Study of Photography in Newspapers* (Lund Humphries 1971).

BERTRAND Claude-Jean, *The British Press. An Historical Survey* (OCDL Paris n.d.). Anthology of Extracts from the press 1622-1967 with a chronological chart.

BONWICK, James, *Early Struggles of the Australian Press* (Gordon and Gotch 1890).

BOURNE, H. R. Fox, *English Newspapers, Chapters in the History of Journalism* (Chatto & Windus 1887).

BOYLE, George, etc. *Newspaper History: From the 17th Century to the Present Day* (Constable 1978).

BRIGHAM, Clarence S., *History and Bibliography of American Newspapers 1690-1820* (American Antiquarian Society 1947).

CAMBRIDGE Bibliography of English Literature (Cambridge University Press 1974-1977). Includes listings of London & provincial newspapers.

CAMROSE, Viscount, *British Newspapers and Their Controllers* (Cassell 1947).

CANADA's Printing Pioneers (Provincial Papers Ltd., Toronto 1966).

CLYDE, William M., *The Struggle for the Freedom of the Press from Caxton to Cromwell* (Humphrey Milford 1934).

COLLET, C. D., *A History of the Taxes on Knowledge* (T. Fisher Unwin, 1899). The story of the struggle for press freedom.

COLLINS, D. E., *A Handlist of News Pamphlets 1590-1610* (S.W. London Technical College 1943).

CRANE, R. S. & KAYE, F. B., *Census of British Newspapers and Periodicals 1620-1800* (Chapel Hill, North Carolina 1927 & reprint).

CRANFIELD, G. A. *A Hand-List of English Provincial Newspapers and Periodicals 1700-1760* (Bowes & Bowes, Cambridge 1952).

CRANFIELD, G. A. *The Development of the Provincial Newspaper 1700-1760* (Oxford University Press 1962).

CUDLIPP, Hugh. Publish and be Damned. *The Astonishing Story of the Daily Mirror* (Andrew Dakers, 1953).

DAHL, Folke. *A Bibliography of English Corantos and Periodical Newsbooks 1620-1642* (Bibliographical Society, 1952).

(DAILY MAIL), *War Despatches from the Pages of the Daily Mail* (Marshall Cavendish 1980).

(DAILY MIRROR), *The Romance of the Daily Mirror 1903-1924. An Illustrated Record* (n.p. 1924).

ESCOTT, T. H. S., *Masters of English Journalism* (T. Fisher Unwin 1911).

FERRIS, Paul, *The House of Northcliffe. The Harmsworths of Fleet Street* (Weidenfeld and Nicolson 1971).

FINCH, Alan, *Pens and Ems, Stories of Australian Newspapers* (Angus & Robertson 1966).

FRANK, Joseph. *The Beginnings of the English Newspaper 1620-1660* (Harvard University Press 1961).

FROST, J., *Great Royal Front Pages* (Collins 1983).

GLENTON, G. & PATTINSON, W., *The Last Chronicle of Bouverie Street* (Allen & Unwin 1963). The Story of the *News Chronicle*.

GOLLIN, Alfred M., *The Observer & J. L. Garvin 1908-1914* (Oxford University Press 1960).

GRAYLAND, Eugene C., *Unusual Newspapers of New Zealand and Australia* (Colenso Collectors' Monographs n.d.).

GREGORY, Winifred, *American Newspapers 1821-1936. A Union List of Files Available in the United States and Canada* (1936, reprinted Kraus 1967).

202

HANDOVER, P. M., *History of the London Gazette 1665-1965* (HMSO 1965).

HANSON, Laurence, *Government and the Press 1695-1763* (Oxford University Press 1936).

HATTON, Joseph. *Journalistic London Being a Series of Sketches of Famous Pens and Papers of the Day* (Sampson Low 1882).

HOBSON, Harold, etc., *The Pearl of Days, An Intimate Memoir of the Sunday Times* 1822-1972 (Hamish Hamilton 1972).

HOLLINS, P., *The Pauper Press* (Oxford University 1970).

HUDSON, Derek, *British Journalists and Newspapers* (Collins 1945).

HUDSON, Frederic, *Journalism in the United States 1690-1872* (Harper, New York 1873).

HUNT, F. Knight, *The Fourth Estate: Contributions Towards a History of Newspapers and the Liberty of Press* (David Bogue 1850).

HUNT, J. R., *Pictorial Journalism* (Pitman 1937).

HURD, Harold, *March of Journalism — Story of the British Press 1622-1952* (Allen & Unwin 1952).

HUTT, Allen, *Newspaper Design* (Oxford University Press 1960).

HUTT, Allen, *The Changing Newspaper. Typographic Trends in Britain and America 1622-1972* (Gordon Fraser 1973).

JACKSON, Mason, *The Pictorial Press, Its Origin and Progress* (Hurst & Blackett 1885).

LINTON, D. & BOSTON, D., *The Press in Britain: an Anthology and Bibliography* (Mansell, projected publication 1985).

(MANCHESTER GUARDIAN), *C. P. Scott. The Making of the Manchester Guardian 1846-1932* (Muller 1946).

MANSFIELD, F. J., *The Complete Journalist. A Study of the Principle and Practice of Newspaper-Making* (Pitman 1935).

MARR, G. S., *The Periodical Essayists of the Eighteenth Century* (James Clark 1923).

McKENZIE, F. A., *The Mystery of the Daily Mail 1896-1921* (Associated Newspapers 1921).

MEYNELL, Francis, *Typography of Newspaper Advertisements* (Ernest Benn 1929).

203

MORISON, Stanley, *The English Newspaper; Some Account of the Physical Development of Journals Printed in London Between 1622 and 1932* (Cambridge University Press 1932). The classic book on typography, layout and development of British newspapers.

MORISON, Stanley, *The Origins of the Newspaper. A Lecture* (St. Bride Institute 1954). Covers the period 1450-1702.

MUNTER, R. L., *A Hand-List of Irish Newspapers 1685-1750* (Bowes & Bowes 1960).

MUNTER, R. L., *The Irish Newspaper 1685-1760* (Cambridge University Press 1967).

(OBSERVER), *The Observer 1791-1921. A Short Record of One Hundred and Thirty Years* (Observer 1921).

PRATT BOORMAN, H. R., *The Newspaper Society. 125 Years of Progress* (Kent Messenger 1961). Histories of provincial newspapers.

(PRESS GUIDES.) *Benn's Newspaper Press Directory. Willing's Press Guide. Writers' and Artists' Year Book.*

Progress of British Newspapers in the Nineteenth Century (Simpkin, Marshall c. 1900). Illustrated throughout with portraits of proprietors and the newspapers they produced.

Red and Black. The Duty and Postage Stamps Impressed on Newspapers 1712-1870 (Times Publishing Co. 1962).

RUST, William, *The Story of the Daily Worker* (People's Press 1949).

SCHOLEFIELD, Guy, *Newspapers in New Zealand* (Reed 1958).

SCOTT, J. W. Robertson, *The Life and Death of a Newspaper* (Methuen 1952). History of the *Pall Mall Gazette*.

SHAABER, M. A., *Some Forerunners of the Newspaper in England 1476-1622* (Frank Cass 1966).

SHEPPARD's Directory of Dealers in Secondhand and Antiquarian Books in the British Isles (Sheppard Press 11th edition 1984).

SMITH, A., *The Newspaper. An International History* (Thames and Hudson 1979).

204

STEWART, J. D., (ed.) *British Union Catalogue of Periodicals* (Butterworth 1955-8).

STOREY, Graham, *Reuters' Century 1851-1951* (Max Parrish 1951).

SYMON, J. D., *The Press and Its Story. An Account of the Birth and Development of Journalism to the Present Day with the History of All the Leading Newspapers* (Seeley, Service 1914).

(THOMASON COLLECTION). *Catalogue of the Thomason Tracts 1640-1661* (British Museum 1908).

TIMES' Handlist: Tercentenary Handlist of English and Welsh Newspapers and Magazines and Reviews (Times Publications 1920). Includes some 20,000 titles 1620-1920.

(THE TIMES). A Newspaper History 1785-1935 (Times Publishing 1935).

WIENER, J. H., *A Descriptive Finding List of Unstamped British Periodicals 1830-6* (Oxford University Press 1970).

WILES, R. M., *Freshest Advices. Early Provincial Newspapers in England* (Ohio State University Press 1965).

WILKINSON-LATHAM, Robert. *From Our Special Correspondent. Victorian War Correspondents and Their Campaigns* (Hodder & Stoughton 1979).

WILLIAMS, J. B., *A History of English Journalism to the Foundation of the Gazette* (Longmans 1908).

WILLIAMS, Keith, *The English Newspaper. An Illustrated History to 1900* (Springwood Books 1977).

WILLIAMS, Neville, *Chronology of the Expanding World 1492-1762* and *Chronology of the Modern World 1763-1966* (Barrie & Rockliffe 1969 & 1966). Events by the month, and also under headings year by year.

WYNN JONES, Michael, *A Newspaper History of the World* (David & Charles 1974).

INDEX

The page numbers in bold type are those of illustrations

210